NEW TRADER RICH TRADER

STEVE BURNS
HOLLY BURNS

DISCLAIMER

This book is meant to be informational and shouldn't be used as trading or investing advice. All readers should gather information from multiple sources to create their personalized investment strategies and trading systems. The authors make no guarantees related to the claims contained herein. Always seek the advice of a competent licensed professional before implementing any plan or system that involves your money. Please invest and trade responsibly.

FOREWORD

When I first met Steve on Twitter, I was curious to know why so many people followed him so faithfully. It didn't take me long to figure it out; Steve is one of the most genuine traders I know.

If you follow him on Twitter, you know he specializes in timeless wisdom and practical trading tips to improve trading results, and that he is ready to lend a helping hand, even if he doesn't know you.

And the book you're about to read is an extension of who he is.

"New Trader, Rich Trader" is a book filled with timeless trading principles. If you're a new trader, it will teach you what works in the market and help reduce your learning curve.

Seasoned traders will be delighted to see that the key principles of trading are reinforced, and they may even have an 'aha' moment that takes their trading to the next level.

Here are some of the things you'll learn in this book:

- How to transition from a new trader to a rich trader
- How to understand the psychology of a professional trader

- How to set expectations; how much can you *really* make trading?
- How to apply quick and easy risk management principles so you don't blow up your account
- How to find a trading methodology that works for you
- What you should look for in a winning trading strategy

What I love most about '*New Trader, Rich Trader*' is the style. Even complicated principles are simple to understand. You will feel like you have a mentor guiding you every step of the way. I know you'll enjoy this book as much as I did!

To your success,
Rayner Teo
http://www.TradingwithRayner.com

PART ONE
PSYCHOLOGY

ONE

New Traders are greedy and have unrealistic expectations;
Rich Traders are realistic about their returns.

WHEN NEW TRADER awoke bright and early, he could feel his excitement building with every second.

Turning on his computer, he thought about all the hard work that went into building his account; all the hours of overtime at his first job, and delivering pizzas on weekends.

That part of his life was now over. His heartbeat quickened as he typed in his username and password. And there it was, his $10,000 trading account.

He was ready.

How could he not be? He had been trading through simulated accounts for over a year, watched financial news, and followed trading gurus online.

The way he saw it, it was easy.

When an account lost too much money, he simply opened a new one. And when he won, his selective memory would choose to forget that the account had also suffered a lot. This fed his ego, convincing him that he could easily outperform the market.

New Trader projected that he could double his account in a few months, then double it again, bringing his account to $40,000 by the end of the year. It would be simple. He had read a few books about legendary traders, and now all he had to do was repeat what they had done.

Unfortunately for New Trader, he didn't understand that these same traders suffered losses and faced difficulties before achieving success. Many had blown up their accounts, some losing 50% or more of their starting capital. Others went bankrupt when they didn't control their risk or ignored their trading plan.

But New Trader wasn't thinking about any of that. He was high on the thought of his $10,000 in buying power. His excitement pushed any fear or doubt to the back of his mind.

He familiarized himself with the platform's tools. Charting software and the trading process on his broker's platform were new to him, but he was eager and hungry to trade.

Now that he was ready, there was only one question left, what to trade?

To reach his initial goal, he knew he would need a stock that would double quickly. Or maybe he should use his entire account and trade one stock three times for a 26% return, each time.

He was good at math and finding solutions to problems. Trading was simply math, and math was simply logic, and New Trader was logical.

Or so he thought.

His head swam thinking about compounded returns; he would be a millionaire in a few years, just like his trading heroes!

One of his heroes, Rich Trader, lived in the same city. New Trader had started visiting him to ask questions about becoming a trader. Maybe he should pay him another visit and get some last-minute advice, not that he needed it, of course.

New Trader soon found himself knocking on Rich Trader's door. They exchanged pleasantries and Rich Trader invited him in.

"I suppose this is about that first account of yours?" Rich Trader said with a wry smile.

"I appreciate you answering my questions," the younger man said. Rich Trader handed a cup of freshly brewed coffee to New Trader and settled into his favorite chair.

New Trader wasted no time. "My plan is to double my account in a few months, and then double it again so I can build it up to $40,000 to trade with next year... what?"

A wide grin had spread across Rich Trader's face as he took a sip of coffee.

"You're planning to be one of the top traders in the world the first year you trade? That's a very aggressive goal for a beginner."

"I just need to find a stock that doubles twice, or have 26% returns compounded three times!" This was the overeager exuberance Rich Trader had come to expect from the younger man.

Rich Trader shook his head, removed his glasses, and rubbed his eyes.

"Well, New Trader," he said after a pause, "while those returns are possible, they typically only happen during special time periods; in the late '20s bull market, or the Internet stock boom of the late '90s, for example. Certain ultra-high growth stocks like Cisco, Google, or Apple did perform incredibly well for long periods of time, but those aren't typical stocks. Not only do you have to find these above average performers, but you must have the right system in place to buy and sell at the right time. That hot stock you're in love with could just as easily fall 50% instead of doubling in price."

He paused to collect his thoughts.

"In addition to all those factors, the market would need to trend in favor of your trading style for you to make those types of returns. It doesn't do any good to plan to buy a stock that's going to double if the market turns bearish and the stock falls. In an economic downturn or when fear takes hold of investors for some reason, they tend to sell just about everything and move their money to safety. Sometimes, this means consumer staple stocks, but it could also be commodities like gold or oil."

When Rich Trader put his glasses back on, he saw that New Trader's hopeful expression had morphed into one of confusion.

"So, you're saying I may not get my 200% return this year?" New Trader asked.

"There is a high probability you will lose money this year," Rich Trader replied matter-of-factly.

"I didn't go through all the trouble of saving money and opening an account to lose! My only purpose is to win," New Trader huffed.

Rich Trader sighed.

"The market will teach you many lessons before you consistently make money. The most dangerous thing you can do is make a lot of money at the beginning. That usually leads to recklessness and big losses in the long run."

"Isn't that what I want to do, win big?" New Trader asked.

"No, you want to get rich slowly. You want to make consistent returns over a long period of time. Your account can grow rapidly by compounding your gains. While you're doing this, you must manage your risk to minimize drawdowns in your equity. Successful trading is based on ever-increasing account equity and minimum drawdowns. Properly managing your account also sets you up for trades that will return 25% during a trend. Your first job as a trader is to focus on building a strong trading system, not dreaming of quick profits."

"Okay, so if I do focus on trading with a system, what returns can I expect?" New Trader was genuinely curious.

"Realistically, a good trader can get a 10% to 25% return or more per year. Some great years can produce 50% returns or more, but those are rare. It's more likely that a trader will lose money the first year, but gain an education. You should look at it like paying tuition. Trading is a profession like any other, and you're trading against professionals most of the time. A surgeon doesn't just read a book and start practicing medicine. They must go to medical school to learn the proper procedures from other doctors. And they will have to practice and make mistakes before they are a paid professional. With surgeons, hopefully their mistakes are made in medical school and not on the operating table!"

New Trader was listening intently.

"Trading is no different." He continued, "I would also assume there's a big difference between operating on a corpse and on a live person during surgery. I'm sure stress comes into play in the operating room, and the doctor must manage stress and have confidence in his skill, as well as his ability to follow the correct procedures. I doubt that a doctor thinks about how much he's getting paid while performing surgery.

You need to focus on a sound strategy, system, and trading plan and not profits. Good trading will create your profits, but focusing on your profits will usually lead to bad trading."

New Trader could feel his agitation and disappointment growing. This advice might have been good for someone else, but he was different. He was smart and had a better feel for the market than other beginning traders. He was the exception. When he finally responded, it was difficult to suppress the contempt he felt.

"So, you think me making a 50% return, or $5,000 in profit this year, is unrealistic?"

Rich Trader could read New Trader like a book and knew what he was thinking, but it didn't bother him. All new traders thought they were special.

"If you did that, you would be in the top 1% of all traders. The bigger question is, are you willing to do the work to beat the other 99%?" Rich Trader asked.

"Absolutely!" New Trader replied, even as he felt his dream of easy money slipping away.

"People who look for easy money invariably pay for the privilege of proving conclusively that it cannot be found on this earth."

JESSE LIVERMORE

Rich Trader's Tip:

My study of profitable, professional traders and money managers leads me to believe that these are the high end of the average annual returns that a successful trader can expect. Achieving this kind of result requires a proven strategy that is followed with discipline.

Recommended reading:

"New Trader 101: The fastest way to grow wealth in the stock market" by Steve Burns and Holly Burns

TWO

New Traders make the wrong decisions because of stress; Rich Traders can manage stress.

NEW TRADER WAS GLUED to his monitor all morning, watching his stock like a hawk.

It went from $9.25 to $9.55, and then back to $9.45. He loved watching the volume climb higher and higher. He loved watching his stock glow bright green while the others were in the red. The Dow Jones was red, and the NASDAQ was clutching to green by barely a tenth of a percent. When his stock hit $9.40, he was ready.

He wanted a thousand shares. He had $10,000 in his account, and he knew this stock could easily rise to $12.00 over the next two months, giving him $2,600 profit. He decided to get in at $9.25; it was showing strong support at $9.00 and hadn't been below that in weeks. Over the past month it had been consistent at around $9.03, but reversed and rallied on high volume before it hit $9.00. In that same period, it had gone as high as $9.89 and stalled there at a new, all-time high.

As the price fell to $9.30, then $9.25, New Trader felt an adrenaline rush as he quickly keyed in the stock symbol, and '1000' beside quantity. Heart pounding, he clicked his mouse and refreshed his trading account screen:

1000 shares SRRS BUY Executed $9.35

"$9.35?!" New Trader shrieked.

Looking at his real-time streamer, he froze. The current quote was $9.10. He felt sick.

"I...I just lost $250?! It takes me an entire weekend of delivering pizzas to make that much." Fear gripped his stomach, wrenching it into a knot.

His heart raced, but this time it was from fear rather than excitement. According to the daily high and low prices, the stock had fallen to $9.08 but had crawled back to $9.15. He tried to calm himself.

"It will hold at $9.00, and climb to $12.00 before earnings. I got in at a great price." He was trying hard to convince himself.

This was entirely different than paper trading and simulations. This was real money, his money. Every cent came from his blood, sweat, and tears, and to have $250 snatched away just like that felt like he'd been robbed.

Why wasn't it going the way he planned? The pressure, stress, and fear he was feeling were much worse than he had anticipated, especially for such a small drop in price.

While he was pulling himself together, the stock rose to $9.40. Despite the $50 in profit, he didn't feel much better. He was gripped by fear of the unknown. He wondered whether to take his profits, or hold until earnings in the next four weeks, as he had originally planned.

He closed his eyes. He could almost see every penny of his

$10,000, perilously crossing a tightrope without a safety net. He felt like it could fall into oblivion at any moment. He had never experienced this level of fear before, and he didn't care for it.

With shaking fingers, New Trader called his mentor, who answered on the third, torturous ring.

"Hello?"

New Trader suddenly felt ashamed, certain that Rich Trader would think he was being foolish. Even so, he managed to force out the words.

"I placed my first trade."

There was a pause, and New Trader could picture the older man smirking.

"That's good..."

"How do you control your stress when trading?" New Trader blurted out.

Rich Trader chuckled, and New Trader wondered why the older man was taking this lightly, this was serious!

"Most stress comes from unknown variables or uncontrolled emotions; fear of loss, uncertainty of market trend, or the need to make money. Sometimes, a trader's ego gets wrapped up in a trade, with their self-worth tied to whether or not they make money," Rich Trader replied.

"But how do you *control* stress?" New Trader urged.

"You can limit your stress level by removing as many unknowns from your system as possible. You should understand your trading plan and a watchlist, and know what you'll buy before you start trading. You must decide how many shares of what stock to trade well before you execute the trade."

Rich Trader cleared his throat and continued.

"Before you place the trade, you need to have an exit strategy of how, when, and why you will take profits and what your stop loss will be. You have to plan to sell your stock at a specific percentage loss, price support breach, or trend change."

"Well, I suppose that makes sense." New Trader's hands had stopped sweating.

"All traders experience stress and must manage it like in any other job. If your stress level is high after you have a trading plan, then you're either trading too big or don't have faith in your system. If you know your system is a winner over time, then try cutting your position size in half. If trading 1,000 shares stresses you out, try trading 500."

"But…" New Trader started, before cutting himself short.

Rich Trader didn't seem to notice the interruption and continued on with his lecture.

"If you're still overwhelmed, go down to 400 or 300 shares per trade. If you think your stress is caused by not having faith in your system, then you need to back test your strategy. Depending on the system and its complexity, this may require back testing your buy and sell signals with computer programs or historical charts. You can also test your method by trading your exact entry and exit signals on paper or in simulators; you will need at least 30 trades spread across different types of markets to get an accurate representation of your potential for success."

"So, I need to make sure I have a system that I follow, design a trading plan that I'm comfortable trading, and I need to test my system to make sure it's a winner, so I'll have faith in my strategy. If I still feel too much pressure, I can decrease my trading size until I'm comfortable."

"Yes, exactly. You need to have a plan to control the outcome of the things that you can control, like stop losses, trailing stops, position size, timing, and technical indicators. You'll need to be comfortable with the volatility of the stock you're trading. Traders need a trading style that's compatible with their personality. More aggressive traders like a stock that moves and gives them a large profit potential. Others like a nice steady, predictable stock. Some love the activity of day trading, while others prefer systems that only need an adjustment a few times a month."

Rich Trader stopped to make sure that the young man was listening.

"The important thing is that you're trading a system that is comfortable for *you* and that it's profitable. If you're stressed out of your mind, then your lack of faith in your system, or your lack of confidence in your knowledge or abilities, are the likely the cause. Alternatively, your position size may be too large for your peace of mind."

"I think I understand, now. Thanks for taking the time to talk to me." New Trader felt a lot better about his prospects.

"Oh, it's no trouble," Rich Trader replied.

New Trader had already identified his problem. A thousand shares were obviously too much for him, and now he knew what he needed to do.

"If you experience high levels of stress during trading, either your position size is too large or you don't have enough confidence in your system. To reduce stress, lower your positions or do more testing on your system."

STEVE BURNS

Rich Trader's Tip:

Trading stress is typically caused by one of two things: either not knowing what to do, or knowing what to do and being too afraid to do it. Only risk 1% of your total trading capital per trade by using stop losses and proper position sizing. Proper position sizing limits the emotional impact of a single trade. Each trade is only one of the next one hundred. If you keep this in mind, it will give you a completely different trading perspective. And remember, if you don't know what to do, don't do anything!

Recommended reading:

"Calm Trader: Win in the stock market without losing your mind" by Steve Burns and Holly Burns

THREE

New Traders are impatient and look for constant action; Rich Traders are patient and wait for entry and exit signals.

NEW TRADER AWOKE two hours before the stock market opened, excited about finally having a weekday off so he could trade.

He made a strong cup of black coffee, signed into his computer, and began to look at the market action in Asia and Europe. All markets were up half a percent on the major indexes. His stock SRRS was at $9.70 in pre-market trading. He grinned and leaned back in his chair. He was up $350 in just one day! He was right, he was a natural!

But first things first, he needed to follow Rich Trader's advice and reduce his position size to something that he felt comfortable with, and create a trading plan that follows a profitable system.

At the market open, he sold 500 shares of SRRS for $9.75 a

share. He made $200 in capital gains minus $20 in commission fees; $10 to buy and $10 to sell. He was happy with the $180 in profits on his first trade. He was still holding the 500 shares of SRRS as earnings approached, and he was within striking distance of his $12 price target.

Rich Trader was right. He did feel a sense of relief now that his position size was smaller. He wasn't experiencing the accelerated heart rate or the level of stress he had felt previously, and concluded that 500 shares, or $5,000 should be his new position size. He thought that as he gained confidence and grew his account, he would be more comfortable with bigger trades. He also hoped to diversify with multiple positions on at the same time. Time would tell.

Now it was time to put the money in his account to work. Because he was trading with a margin account instead of a cash account, he could place a trade today and not have to wait three days for it to clear.

He felt comfortable with his new trading plan of a 500-share position of $5,000. If a stock was $50, he would trade 100 shares. If a stock was $5, he would trade 1,000 shares. He reasoned that he also might need to factor in the volatility of a stock. He wanted to trade stable stocks in uptrends. He would trade stocks with no more than a 5% daily price range. He went online and checked his SRRS' price history. It was a volatile stock, averaging a little less than 5% a day in price movement.

This didn't stress New Trader because he wanted a stock with movement. He needed some volatility to show him the movement of the trend, to make a profit, and to cover his trading costs. He wondered if 5% movement was too volatile. With a 50% position in total capital, a 5% move against him would be a 2.5% loss of trading capital. This was something to keep in mind.

With financial news playing in the background, and the live streamers flashing by on his screen, he was ready to start building his trading plan.

He glanced back at his position; his stock was now at $9.92; it had broken through the 52-week high. This made him happy. He felt a sense of satisfaction knowing that he picked a winner and purchased it at a good entry point. But then he started to question his motives. Why did he buy at that price? Was it because it was at a short-term price support level? Was it a hunch? Did he really have a system that he traded, or was he just a random, discretionary trader relying on his opinions?

He had trouble finding answers to these questions. He also had an overwhelming desire to put the other $5,000 in his account to work. He looked at his watchlist for action. The market was now up almost 1% across most indexes, and DMY, a supplier to SRRS, was at a new 52-week high of $4.90. He didn't hesitate; he bought 1,000 shares of DMY at $4.91. The stock then went to $4.95, then stalled and reversed to $4.92. He was hoping for a strong upward trend for profits.

While he watched the bid/ask spread hang around the $4.92/$4.93 mark, he started to question himself. What was he doing? He had no exit strategy. He had no idea why he had just bought those shares!

He didn't realize it at the time, but greed was his motivator, and in the future, it was going to ask him to make some bad decisions.

Maybe trying to create a trading plan during trading hours wasn't the best idea.

After staring at the screen for thirty minutes waiting for the stock to do something, he decided to sell. He sold 1,000 shares for $4.92. He was relieved that he didn't lose any money on the trade, until he noticed that his account had gone down by an extra $10. To his surprise, he realized that his profit was $10, but he had paid $20 in commissions on the trade!

He felt foolish for having made that trade in the middle of creating a trading plan, and decided to call Rich Trader.

When Rich Trader answered the phone, New Trader got right to the point.

"Have you ever made a trade without knowing why you did it?"

"Yes, when I was much younger, when the stakes were high and my adrenaline got pumping, I did things I regretted." Rich Trader said.

"What causes overtrading or spontaneous trading?"

Rich Trader paused and reflected before replying.

"Well, it can be caused by a number of things, including not having a solid trading plan, getting impatient, looking for excitement, or being arrogant and thinking that you're smarter than other traders."

"And what can I do to stop this?" New Trader was distressed, and he was sure his voice reflected his duress.

"I would suggest that you trade only to make money, not for entertainment or to prove something to yourself. Profitable trading is often boring. If you already know what you're going to do before you trade, it takes a lot of the excitement out of it. If you have a trading plan and a good system in place, there are no spontaneous trades. You will spend your time waiting for entry signals and exit signals. You will learn that your system makes you money in the long-term, but your ego loses you money in the short term. Trade your system and not your opinions."

"That makes a lot of sense..."

"Do your planning and research while the market is closed; trade your system while the market is open."

"I still have a lot to learn. Thanks for listening."

"Experience will be your greatest teacher," Rich Trader replied.

New Trader decided not to place more trades until he had a plan.

"It's better to do nothing than to do what is wrong. For whatever you do, you do to yourself."

BUDDHA

Rich Trader's Tip:

Objective traders have a quantified method, system, rules, and principles that they use to trade. They get in a trade based on facts, and where they get out is based on price action. Objective traders have a written trading plan to guide them. They use objective historical price action, charts, probabilities, risk management, and their edge. They react to what is happening only if it can be quantified. They go with the flow of price action, and not the flow of their emotions.

Don't attach your ego to your trades. Be the trader that witnesses the trade from an emotional distance, with respect and curiosity. If you can put space between yourself and the trade, you will become more accurate and more profitable.

Recommended reading:

"Buy Signals, Sell Signals: Strategic stock market entries and exits" by Steve Burns and Holly Burns

FOUR

New Traders trade because they are influenced by their own greed and fear; Rich Traders use a trading plan.

NEW TRADER FELT MORE prepared than ever before. It was time to get serious; it was time to start creating a trading plan. But first he had to answer some questions.

Taking one of his favorite trading books off the shelf, he opened it to the chapter on how to write a trading plan. He decided to make notes and answer the questions as he went.

What is your signal for entering a trade?

He decided he would trade trends, so his signal needed to buy into price strength and increasing volume. Instead of buying support, he would buy at the break to a new high, or when it breaks resistance of a moving average or price.

When will you sell?

When did he plan to sell SRRS? If he had a stop loss, he needed a plan to take profits.

Twelve dollars was his target, but what if it only goes to $11.99 and then reverses? Would he be ridiculous enough to give back his profits and maybe even lose money if it kept falling, even below his purchase price? He thought the best plan would be to trail a stop loss and take profits if it pulled back 5%. If it went up steadily to $9.85, then pulled back to $9.35, he would get out even.

If it went all the way to $11.99, then pulled back to $11.19, he would get out with a nice profit. He would avoid giving back all his profits and have a plan to sell. However, the stock would need a nice uptrend for this system to work. He knew that in a bull market it should do well. It would allow profits to run and prevent too many stop losses when the stock moved in its normal price range.

How much will you risk on each trade?

He decided to risk only 2% of his trading account per trade. This would significantly reduce the risk of ruin he had read about so often. If he traded a $5,000 position, he would only risk $200 of his trading capital; with a 500-share position, that would be 40 cents a share. His stop on his SRRS trade should be at $8.95, since he bought it at $9.35 and still had 500 shares.

What will your trade size be?

He decided that his trade size would be $5,000 and however many shares that would buy of any one stock.

What equities will you trade?

He would trade in the hottest stocks in the market, with at least one million shares traded a day for liquidity. They would need a daily range of less than 4%.

How long will you hold your trades?

His plan was to hold stocks as long as he could while they went up without pulling back in price. A price breakout could fail, forcing him to sell on the first day and make him a day trader. Or he could also end up holding a stock for over a year, it never pulling back after going into a trend, giving it a chance to rocket upwards. He would put 2%, or $200, at risk in each trade with unlimited upside.

How will you test your system for profitability?

The only way to test his system was to study historical charts, paper trade, or use a simulator; but his stock picking was too subjective and discretionary to program into software.

What is expected risk/reward ratio?

Trading at this size with this tight of an initial stop loss could cause him to be stopped out because of volatility. His entries would have to be incredibly accurate, but he would be rewarded because the best stocks can run up to 15% or more before earnings. Some stocks can go up 50% or even double before their trend changes.

This would give him a chance to cash in on the winners, but his buys would need to be precise and disciplined. He couldn't afford to miss a stock, have it run 4% in an uptrend, and then chase the stock and buy it late. In a volatile stock that moves a lot during the day, it would be crucial that it was in an uptrend and didn't pullback enough to get him stopped out.

He decided to put in a buy stop so that the stock would be automatically bought at the beginning of an uptrend.

New Trader felt confident in his trading plan. He had followed suggestions from the many trading books and the advice from Rich Trader. He didn't feel the need to bother Rich Trader again. He had pestered him enough, and he felt like he had a handle on it. He was beginning to feel like a businessman writing a business plan. This feeling was a lot different than the adrenaline rush he got from trading with size, based on his opinions.

He wondered if his plan was not aggressive enough. Maybe he should be taking more risk. Was $200 a trade worth all this trouble?

His greed wanted a more aggressive trading plan; it wanted to be a millionaire in a year, not trade for a few hundred dollars. Greed wasn't the least bit interested in him getting rich slowly. And as he began to feel tempted by a more aggressive trading plan, fear and doubt started gnawing at him.

What if he lost his first ten trades in a row? That would be $2,000 gone. He had worked hard for that money. It could take him four or five months to save that much again! He felt nauseous.

"Was it worth it?" he said aloud, thinking about his job, and then his second job.

He remembered the millionaire trading legends he had read about, and the freedom that Rich Trader enjoyed. Rich Trader had a nice home, no boss, no schedule, and no traffic. And he had become a millionaire even though he was a college dropout!

New Trader had to decide. Would he give up and go back to working at a job for the rest of his life, or would he follow the path to wealth as a trader? When he put it like that, the choice seemed simple. He would be a trader. What other job offered this kind of opportunity, freedom, and these odds of success? It was like a lottery he could win based on hard work and discipline.

"Pride is a great banana peel – as are hope, fear, and greed. My

biggest slip ups occurred shortly after I got emotionally involved with positions."

ED SEYKOTA

Rich Trader's Tip:

Successful traders have a plan for success. By carefully putting the odds in their favor, successful traders will overtake gamblers who rely on random trades and prayers. If you want to win in life, you must study, work hard, and be disciplined. There are no short cuts, and especially not in trading. You need to enter the markets well prepared, with a detailed trading plan, and weather the storm.

Recommended reading:

"How to Make Money in Stocks Getting Started: A Guide to Putting CAN SLIM Concepts into Action" by Matthew Galgani

FIVE

New Traders are unsuccessful when they stop learning; Rich Traders never stop learning about the market.

NEW TRADER WOKE up feeling like he had finally done it. He was a good trader. He had his style and his trading plan. It was Saturday and the markets were closed, so he decided to call Rich Trader to see if he was available to grab a quick bite to eat. It was time to relax and enjoy his profits.

They agreed to meet, and before noon they were sitting in a cozy restaurant ordering breakfast.

"I have this trading thing figured out," New Trader said randomly while enjoying his scrambled eggs.

Rich Trader nearly spit out his orange juice

"What's so funny?" New Trader asked, putting down his fork and staring at his mentor.

"I'm sorry," Rich Trader said as he finally caught his breath. "I just don't think I've ever heard anyone say that before."

"I've done a lot of research, and decided on my style: trend trading. I've also written my trading plan," he said, handing Rich Trader a folded piece of paper with one hand, and eating a piece of bacon with the other. He loved bacon.

Rich Trader looked it over carefully. "This is a great start."

"Start?" New Trader said incredulously.

"This is like you're turning in your first freshman paper. If you're like other successful traders, you will have to test this system first and then make adjustments." Rich Trader took another sip of orange juice.

"It may work well for a while, then suddenly stop working and give your capital a large drawdown due to a change in market conditions. The system may not even work, you don't know yet. Or it might make you a nice profit in a bull market then take the profits back in a bear market. If you want to be profitable in a bear market, you may have to reverse your system and sell the same stocks short when they break down through support. Testing your system in back tests and real time will teach you a lot. First you need to get an idea of your winning percentage and the average size of your wins and losses."

New Trader could feel the confidence and his appetite fading. Why was trading so complicated? He hadn't even considered the possibility that creating his system would be the beginning and not the end of his trading education. Despite what he had hoped, this meeting with Rich Trader wasn't going to be any different than the others; he always came confident and left humbled.

"You're saying that my next step is system testing and making adjustments?" New Trader asked, attempting to hide his disappointment.

"Yes, your system is built on solid principles, but you need to quantify and measure them as much as possible. You need to build a record of how the system performs in real trades. But most importantly, you need to test your discipline and confidence in trading the system exactly as you planned," Rich Trader informed him.

"Of course I will!" New Trader said defensively.

Rich Trader raised a brow.

"I would also urge you to keep a trading journal. Use it to list your trades and to record any problems you have in your own ability to buy or sell at the right times, based on your trading plan and system. Record breaches of discipline and why you traded off the plan. You must always be watchful of an inflated ego taking over your trading, and be on the lookout for greed and fear. Boredom can turn good traders into bad traders, because they look for action instead of following a process. A trading journal is like having a teacher who teaches traders about themselves."

New Trader almost said that he thought it was a silly waste of time, but he knew Rich Trader had his best interests at heart, and he hadn't been wrong so far.

"What will my journal show me?"

"Patterns." Rich Trader said flatly.

"What kind of patterns?"

"You will be able to see what is causing your good trades and your bad trades. What you were thinking and what caused you to go against your plan. Also, what made your best trades possible. You might even see patterns that show your system works best in the morning, or in the final two hours of trading. In addition to your technical trading information, be sure you note your mood, feelings, and goals. Include your charts with buy and sell areas marked, as often as possible."

"I'll do that," said New Trader as he picked at his last pancake.

"Are there any other lessons you think are important?" New Trader asked.

"Always stay humble. Always know the market is too big for anyone to master. You must never stop learning about yourself, about the market, and about risk," Rich Trader said before posing a question, "How many trading books have you read?"

"Ten," New Trader said.

"Most of the best traders have read hundreds," Rich Trader said. "How long do you spend looking at charts each day?"

"A few minutes before I place a trade." New Trader knew that wasn't a good answer.

"Great traders spend hours a day doing homework on back testing, chart studies, identifying support, resistance, and trends," Rich Trader informed his student. "Great traders are life-long learners. My advice is to always be a student of the market, always go to bed each night understanding more than you did when you woke up. With hard work, experience, and focus, you will one day convert all of that time into money."

"In my whole life, I have known no wise people over a broad subject matter area who didn't read all the time – none, zero."

CHARLIE MUNGER

Rich Trader's Tip:

Trading systems are built for an individual's risk tolerance and personality type, but the principles used to build trading systems are basically the same. You must choose if your system will be profitable from a high win rate, or big wins and small losses. And you must eliminate the possibility of large losses in your trading system by implementing the risk management tools of stop losses, option contracts, futures contracts, and position sizing.

Recommended reading:

"How Legendary Traders made Millions" by John Boik

PART TWO
RISK

SIX

New Traders act like gamblers; Rich Traders operate like businesspeople.

NEW TRADER TURNED off his phone alarm as soon as it went off. He had been lying awake for some time, thinking about his breakfast meeting with Rich Trader. It was an hour before the market opened and he needed to prepare. He felt the shot of adrenaline he got every time he traded, and he rushed to turn on the financial news.

The European and Asian markets were up over 1%, and though he tried to understand the numbers they were rattling off, he couldn't decipher exactly why the markets were up. But he could see that the traders were bullish, and prices were moving upward.

Confident he would be making money that day, he laid his trading plan beside his computer. He spent two weeks after that breakfast with Rich Trader testing his system and recording signals for ten test trades.

- Trade 1: -$250 loss
- Trade 2: -$250 loss
- Trade 3: $250 gain
- Trade 4: Even
- Trade 5: $500 profit
- Trade 6: -$250 loss
- Trade 7: $200 gain
- Trade 8: $750 gain
- Trade 9: $300 gain
- Trade 10: $400 gain

With seven wins and three losses (when you don't lose money it's a win; you only pay the expense of the commission), he had made $2,400, and lost $750, for a profit of $1,650. His system seemed to work well, but he knew Rich Trader would tell him it took more than ten trades to define a system's long-term viability, and that the market being in an uptrend could be the reason for his success.

He was glad that he had taken Rich Trader's advice, and he reviewed his journal to remind him of all he had learned.

Cutting losses was crucial; many of the stocks he sold with a $250 loss continued to fall and he could have lost over $1,000 on one of them. He needed to know the amount of money he was willing to risk before he placed a trade.

Automatic buy stops were good because it helped him make extra money by getting into a trade automatically. If he had attempted to buy some of these stocks in an uptrend, he would have lost hundreds of dollars in profits while trying to buy it manually.

He took a profit when it began to fall. If he didn't have a trailing stop, he would have given back all his profits on two of the trades. It's good to have a profit-taking strategy.

He thought his system would be better if he found a way to buy earlier in a hot stock, maybe at support, and take profits on a big run up instead of on a drawdown. He would ask Rich Trader about that.

New Trader felt a strong urge to trade in the markets that morning, so he decided to scan his watchlist for buy points. His greed, like a cartoon devil on his shoulder, whispered into his ear and told him to buy the stock with real money, instead of the simulated account. He deserved it, didn't he? He had worked hard and he deserved the profits. The market owed him.

The real-time streamers flashed red and green, calling to him like the Las Vegas lights tempt gamblers. For a moment the little devil won, and the desire for a big win and easy money filled his thoughts. He was clever, and he could beat the market. Stocks were going up. He only had his one SRRS position on, and it was now at $10.35 with paper profits of $500. He was encouraged, and decided that he would sell if it retraced to $9.85.

He shook his head and looked down at his desk. He needed to stay on track. It would be foolish to buy a stock with no plan. It was time to get away from the computer and the temptation to trade. He called Rich Trader and received an invitation to come by and visit.

When New Trader showed up around noon, it occurred to him that he never saw Rich Trader watching financial news, nor did Rich Trader have a fancy trading desk with multiple monitors. New Trader wondered if he was still actively trading, or if he had retired.

"I am surprised at the temptations I feel when I trade," New Trader began. "I always want to trade aggressively instead of following my plan."

"Like all businesses and disciplines, the psychological aspect is usually the most difficult," Rich Trader said. "Being a professional means doing your job no matter how you feel. A trader has two jobs; you're a researcher and a trader. First, you must do your research. You need to find systems that have a good probability of success in the long-term, test those systems, and create a trading plan that fits your personality. Decide the correct amount of risk to take on for each trade, based on your winning percentage and historical drawdown. Then your job is to follow that plan and not change it during market hours, no matter how you feel. Adjustments should only be made in off hours."

"Drawdown?" New Trader asked, feeling a bit foolish.

"A trading account doesn't go straight up. You may start with $10,000, go down to $9,500, then go up to $10,500. Even if you eventually double your account, it may be a choppy uptrend. You could have a big win followed by three small losses, then another big win, and then two small losses. That's normal. The key to success is to lose small and win big," Rich Trader said.

"When you're in a loser, get out; the best trades make money at the buy point. When you're winning, let it run until it stops. You will lose if you don't cut your losses, hoping against hope that they will come back. And you won't be successful if you panic and take quick profits and miss out on the bigger wins that will pay for your losses."

"There is also one more, very important, thing," Rich Trader added after a moment. "When you go to your computer to trade, you should approach it as if you're entering an auction, not a casino. You should feel like you're going to work for your own business, not like you're playing a slot machine or spinning a roulette wheel. If you experience these feelings, or you just want to gamble, you will eventually fail as a trader.

Trend traders make money, chart readers make money, swing traders make money, day traders make money, and position traders make money, but all gamblers in the market eventually lose everything."

When Rich Trader finished, New Trader felt a little unsettled, but he took the warning to heart.

"Risk comes from not knowing what you're doing."

WARREN BUFFETT

Rich Trader's Tip:

Many people think they are traders when they trade more like gamblers who would probably have better odds if they went to Las Vegas. The difference between a trader and a gambler is like the difference between a casino and a gambler. The casino paradigm introduced in Trade like a Casino by Richard Weissman can help new traders think differently and become profitable.

The casino doesn't risk it all on a single game, their table limits ensure that a single win doesn't impact their overall profitability. A casino also doesn't have emotions. It doesn't care about the players or whether they're winning or losing. In contrast, the gambler can become consumed by emotion. A gambler usually has a problem taking their winnings off the table after a streak; they may win sometimes, but gamblers will usually lose in the end.

Be the casino.

Recommended reading:

"Trade Like a Casino" by Richard Weissman

SEVEN

New Traders bet the farm; Rich Traders carefully control trading size.

NEW TRADER WAS deep in thought. He wanted more profits and he wanted them to come more quickly. Maybe now that he had experienced holding 500 shares of SRRS for almost a month he was ready to trade 1,000 shares. He would exchange one position of $10,000 instead of two positions of $5,000.

He assumed that now that he had $20,000 with the use of margin, he would be comfortable trading $10,000. He worked it over in his mind, trying to convince himself to change his trading plan. He wanted a big trading account, and his current pace was going to take too long. He reasoned that SRRS was going to $12 by the time its earnings were announced, and this prediction propelled him to go all in.

He realized that greed was getting the better of him again, and he tried to focus on Rich Trader's lessons.

"Your first job as a trader is to focus on the correct trading process, not profits."

Profits would come to him one trade at a time. Then he had an idea, something that hadn't occurred to him before. SRRS $11 call options for next month were trading at $1 a contract. He could control 10,000 shares for his $10,000. He knew that option contracts were for 100 shares, and that the quote price is for each share, so paying $100 to control 100 shares seemed straightforward.

What he didn't understand was that the stock had to go up to $11, *plus* the cost of the option premium. SRRS had to go up to $12 in 30 days, just to break even. He wasn't buying intrinsic value, he was buying $1 in *time* value, with the stock trading at around $10. He was purchasing the right to have the shares at that price, for one month. He didn't realize how unlikely is was that the stock would go up 20 percent in 30 days. Historically, SRRS moved between 10 and 15 percent leading up to, or after each earnings announcement, and that had already occurred.

There were significant problems with New Trader making this trade:

- It was against his trading plan.
- He didn't understand the nature of what he would be trading.
- He had not researched the history of the stock's price, so he didn't know the potential for failure.
- It was an all-or-nothing bet. If the options expired worthless, he would lose his entire trading account.

Even if he was correct about the trade and made a large profit, it would encourage him to take the risk again. If he continued to make risky trades, he would eventually lose his entire account.

Fortunately for him, his trepidation caused him to listen to another one of his emotions – Fear. Fear can cripple a trader, but it's also helpful if you have enough fear to keep you safe from greed. Fear was very quick to point out that he could lose everything if this trade was a complete loss. His fear also prevented him from calling Rich Trader to tell him about his compulsion to roll the dice and bet the farm.

And that's when it hit him. If he was too embarrassed to talk a trade over with his trading mentor, it's not a trade he should be making. New Trader decided to go to his mentor's home for advice on improving his trading plan and making it more in line with his goals. But he also decided not to tell Rich Trader about his bout with fear and greed.

He arrived at Rich Trader's house unannounced in the middle of the weekday, and was surprised to see him answer the door in pajamas with a book in hand. How odd, New Trader thought to himself. Why wasn't he watching the financial news? Why wasn't he at his desk, glued to his monitor?

New Trader was curious. "Are you doing any trading today?" he asked, leaning awkwardly on the door frame. Rich Trader motioned the young trader inside.

"I have some trailing stops in, so if my positions reverse, I'll be sold out. I'm going to check in at the last hour of trading to see if I should enter any additional buy stops." Rich Trader slipped his book back onto the bookcase and sat down.

New Trader was dumbfounded. He didn't understand how Rich Trader, with an account his size, doing this for a living, could be so blasé about his trading? So disconnected? Why wasn't he following every tick? Why wasn't he watching everything that happened in the markets?

"Aren't you concerned about your positions, or about missing any trading opportunities?" New Trader asked.

"Well, we all hate to lose money, but my sells are based on hitting predetermined stop losses and not my opinions. I also trade a system, not my predictions about what the market will do. So there's no need to sit at my desk or watch financial news all day, because those things could cause me to be impulsive and make trades that go against my trading plan."

"I was tempted to take a trade against my trading plan today, but chose not to," admitted New Trader. So much for not telling his mentor.

"Well, the most dangerous part of your plan to ignore is your risk. Trading a larger position puts your account at greater risk," said Rich Trader.

"That's what I was tempted to do." New Trader said sheepishly.

"If you make a mistake and lose a few percentage points of your account, that's not a big a deal, you can trade and get that back. You can lose 5% of your account four times in a row and be down 20%, so you need to gain 25% to be even again." He paused in thought. "Of course, normally these are spread out. For example, two wins and then a loss. Then three wins and two losses, et cetera.

The problems start when you make large, reckless trades without taking your planned stop loss, and end up losing 50% of your account. Then you must gain 100% to get back to even. If a 50% loss takes your $10,000 account to $5,000, you need to gain 100% on your new $5,000 in capital to get back to $10,000. That is a disaster. If you go from $10,000 to $8,000 with a 20% loss, a 25% return will take you back to $10,000. The greatest determiner of your risk is the size of your trade.

I would never risk more than a 1% loss on any trade, maybe 2% if I wanted to be aggressive and go for larger returns. The more aggressively you pursue returns through exposing your account to risk, the greater the likelihood of larger drawdowns in capital. Good trades are generally ones which show a profit from the beginning."

New Trader let it all sink in.

"I was going with 5% as my stop loss with 2.5% percent of my total account at risk." He squeaked.

"And what is your expected gain for your wins?"

"I don't know." He suddenly felt like he was in over his head.

Rich Trader shook his head. "That's very important, you must know the answer to that question. Out of ten trades, if you take a 2% loss of total trading capital five times, and your five wins are only 1% returns on your capital, you're still down 5% on your account on ten trades with bad risk/reward ratios. However, if you lose 5% five times and then gain 10% five times, you're up 25% after ten trades that are the same position size with a 50%-win rate. But, if you don't keep consistent position sizes and good risk/reward ratios, you will distort your payoff ratio."

"Payoff ratio?" New Trader asked with wide eyes.

"Basically, the ratio of the average winning trade to the average losing trade. The larger this ratio is, the better chance you'll have a winning strategy. It's difficult to be a successful trader with a payoff ratio under 1.5. The ratio is calculated by dividing the gross profits by the gross losses. Most traders want at least $2 of reward for every $1 at risk. Which is what the 5% loss versus a 10%-win scenario with a 50%-win ratio gave you in our second example.

It's critical that when you're testing and trading your system, you keep track of your winning percentage and payoff ratio, so you can have accurate profit expectations. It's also crucial to develop faith in your system so you can continue trading it, even when it's losing. All systems go through drawdowns, times when market conditions are not conducive to profits based on the style of your system."

"Hmm... I see. Thanks again, Rich Trader. You've shown me some things I need to examine carefully while I develop my system and trading plan. I still have a lot of work to do."

"Anytime, New Trader," said Rich Trader, as he showed the younger man out. "But next time, would you mind calling first?"

"It's not whether you're right or wrong that's important, but how much money you make when you're right and how much you lose when you're wrong."

GEORGE SOROS

Rich Trader's Tip:

An important, and often overlooked trading dynamic, is the importance of taking trades that have the potential to be big wins or small losses. Big losses will deplete your account quickly, and small wins will do little to pay for those losses. Trades need to be asymmetric. The downside is carefully planned and managed, but the upside is open-ended. This is an important element of successful trading.

Recommended reading:

"A Trader's Money Management System: How to Ensure Profit and Avoid the Risk of Ruin" by Bennett McDowell

EIGHT

For New Traders, large profits are the #1 priority; for Rich Traders, managing risk is the #1 priority.

NEW TRADER FOUND himself knocking on Rich Trader's door early the next morning. Rich Trader opened the door after a few minutes.

"Hello, again," Rich Trader said in his usual, even tone. "You called this time, at least."

New Trader grinned. "I've come for class, Professor."

"I'm afraid I don't have a lecture prepared today, but why don't you come in, have a seat and tell me what's on your mind. Perhaps I can help."

"Well, managing risk seems to be much more important than I thought."

"Risk is like a wild dog, and it can bite a trader in many ways.

Different trading methods expose you to different kinds of risk."

"I thought risk was just the chance that you could lose money?"

"It is, but there are many ways you can lose money."

New Trader settled in.

"First, you have the risk that your trade will be a loss, and that it will move in the opposite direction of your long or short position. This is your standard trade risk. However, you can typically control the maximum amount you lose through position size and a stop loss.

You also have the general market risk factor. You can pick the stock of an amazing company, but if the trend of the stock market itself is down for some reason, it's likely that your stock will also fall. Regardless of the fundamental merits of the company or the past strength of your stock's price movement, nothing is guaranteed. The market is like a tide that comes in, it lifts up all ships, and when it goes out again, it lowers them back down.

You have the risk of your stock either being, or becoming, highly volatile. Volatility risk can scare you into selling your stock too soon, or cause your system to stop working because the stock hit your predetermined stop loss and forced you to sell.

Overnight risk is when something unexpected happens while the market is closed, and the next morning your stock gaps down in the pre-market, never giving you a chance to sell and stop your loss. This risk applies to everyone except day traders, or those who trade futures markets that are open almost 24 hours a day.

Liquidity risk is when there are not many buyers or sellers for your stock, so you lose money in the bid/ask spread. The "bid" is what they are willing to buy your stock for, and the "ask" is how much they are offering to sell it for. There are stocks and options which have very low volume, and they can lose 5%-10% or more by being bought and sold, even if the stock price doesn't move. If your stock has a bid of $9.50 and an ask of $10.00, and you buy it at the ask price and then sell it at the bid price, you lose 5% on entry and 5% on exit. It's important to trade in stocks that have a small spread in the bid/ask quotes. Less than .10 is good, but a penny or two is ideal.

Margin risk is when a trader uses stock as collateral to borrow money from their broker to buy additional stocks. After you have set up a margin account, most brokers will let you buy additional stocks and double the size of your account. With margin, you can use a $10,000 account to buy $20,000 worth of stock if the stocks are marginable securities. Risky penny stocks and small cap stocks are not marginable, or can only be margined for a smaller percentage. You can make twice as much profit when you're right, but you can lose twice as much if you're wrong. This increases your risk of ruin by making your losses compound twice as fast!

If you're holding a stock through earnings, you're exposed to the risk of a sharp move in one direction after the announcement, and this is an earnings risk. Your account can suffer if the move is too fast after hours and gaps through your stop loss.

Political Risk can affect you if you're invested in a company located in a different country, or your stock's company does business in a country that is unstable or has a change in power. For example, investors and property owners in Cuba were wiped out when the Communists took over all private property in 1960.

If you trade options, the clock is always ticking against you, and this is the risk of time decay. A major component of a stock option's value is its time value. It loses a small amount of this value every day until it's only worth is the intrinsic worth; how much it's 'in the money' based on its strike price. An options trader must be right about the price movement and the time frame. They are also paying for the right to control the shares, so to be a winning trade, they must be on the right side of price movement by more than the extrinsic cost of the stock.

Technology risk is one of the most frustrating things a trader can experience. Internet connection issues or your broker's trading plat-form going down in the middle of a trade will happen sooner or later, so it's a good idea to have a backup plan in place. Have the phone number for your broker, or multiple brokers, ready so you can get out of a trade in an emergency. Having redundant Internet access across multiple devices is also advisable.

And then there's the risk of good old fashioned human error. You could put one too many zeroes on your buy order, or buy the wrong symbol, or sell a stock short instead of buying it. Double checking your trades before you place them is a critical component to a trader's success."

When Rich Trader finished, New Trader was deep in thought for several minutes. Finally, he replied.

"That's a little overwhelming. It's amazing to me that you can talk about all of that off the top of your head."

"You learn to respect risk as a trader. Before you start any trading system you must look at all the risks involved. Ask yourself questions like, 'How much am I willing to risk per trade?' and 'If I lose five times in a row, what will be my drawdown in capital?'"

"Can you give me any suggestions on managing these different types of risk?"

Rich Trader nodded.

"Here are some simple suggestions to help lower your risks when you trade. Some of this you have probably heard before:

- Determine your stop loss before you place a trade.
- Honor your stop and cut your loss.
- Balance your wins and losses by trading the same position size in capital on every trade.
- Only make trades that meet the criteria of your predetermined trading plan.
- Trade primarily long in uptrending bullish markets, and mostly short in downtrending bearish markets, or go to cash. A 10-day moving average over the 50-day moving average is a good sign of an uptrend, and the reverse is a sign of potential bearishness.
- Only use margin to trade more trades of equal size. You won't typically have to wait three days for your trade to

clear to get your buying power back, and you can keep trading after trades are closed. Don't use margin to make one large trade, but instead use it to create a quicker turn around on your capital.

- Only trade in stocks with over a million or more shares traded daily. Only trade options with open interest of over a thousand contracts.

- You can avoid overnight risk as a day trader, but the most profitable traders carry trades for weeks and months. You can mitigate overnight risk by going to cash when an announcement, like company earnings, is to be delivered after hours.

- Manage volatility risk by trading slow, dependable stocks which have consistent daily ranges. A stock with a beta of 1.0 moves the same as the S&P 500. A stock with a beta of 2.0 moves twice as fast as the index. You want to trade lower beta stocks to manage volatility. You don't need a volatile stock to make money, you need a stock that is either in a trend, or in a price range with support and resistance levels.

- You can control political risk by trading stocks that do most of their business in countries with historically stable governments, such as the United States, United Kingdom, Canada, and Japan, rather than emerging markets

- You can limit the risk of time decay with options by trading deep in the money calls and puts. Most of these are pure intrinsic value and have little time value, if any. So even though they cost more, you eliminate the risk of time running out before they go in the money.

- Remember to double check trade information before you hit enter. I have accidentally traded 10,000 shares instead of 1,000. I have also traded a stock long when I meant to short it.

- Have a Plan B for your broker and Internet connection. I always keep my broker's number as a favorite on my cellphone, and I've setup a 'hot spot' mobile Internet connection so I can get online quickly if my home network goes down."

"I never really thought about all the risks involved. Those are all great tips. Thanks for my lesson," New Trader said, getting up to leave.

"I am always happy to help," Rich Trader said pleasantly, but he was feeling a little drained. He did a lot of talking, and he hoped that New Trader took good notes.

"Rule #1: Never lose money. Rule #2: Never forget rule #1."

WARREN BUFFETT

Rich Trader's Tip:

I never want to lose more than 1% on any one trade. If I am trading with a $100,000 account, I don't want to lose more than $1,000 in a losing trade. A stop loss level should start at the price level that you know you will be proven wrong, and work back to position sizing. If you're only risking 1% of your trading capital when you're wrong, every trade can become just one of the next 100, with little emotional or financial impact. You will survive losing streaks and increase your odds of long-term success.

Recommended reading:

"Super Trader" by Van Tharp

NINE

New Traders try to prove they are right; Rich Traders admit when they are wrong.

NEW TRADER STUMBLED to his computer. He was tired. He had been holding SRRS for over a month and it was behaving well. It climbed up to a new all-time high of $10.58 before falling back to $10.03. He was proud of himself and confident his stock would rise to $12, just as he had predicted.

He was moving slow this morning, but after sitting down and booting up, he was quickly in his brokerage account and ready for action. He glanced at his real-time ticker and stood up to make some coffee. He froze, and his stomach did a slow roll as he sat back down.

$9.25.

The pre-market quote was $9.25! He was now wide awake, no coffee needed.

"$9.25? What the..."

He quickly worked through the math. At one time he was up $615, and now he was down $50?! His profits had evaporated overnight. He did an online search and found that one of SRRS's rivals had announced that it was bringing a digital device to market that was superior to SRRS's. Analysts believed it would be available in less than four months, and that SRRS would lose 20% market share in the first year.

New Trader was numb, so his ego stepped in to help with his trading plan. What should he do? His ego cooed, "Don't worry, you're right, just hold the position. The stock will come back. The other company's product can't be as good as the original. This is just a knee-jerk reaction from other traders."

New Trader thought that his ego was probably right, but he couldn't bear to think about all the wasted time and effort over the last few months if this didn't turn around. If he didn't sell, he wasn't wrong, not yet. He would have to be patient and wait for the rally. Then he would sell.

New Trader's trading plan, unlike his ego, was neutral. His ego said be patient, but his trading plan said 'Sell'. The trading plan was created to protect New Trader from large losses, or from giving back too much of his profits. Unfortunately, New Trader believed he was smarter than the trading plan. He chose to forget that he had planned to sell when the stock retraced 5%, it had retraced over 10%, and he still wasn't convinced to sell.

He was now emotionally invested in these returns. He was attached to them; he had been fawning over them daily for weeks. They were his, and he would get them back. Not surprisingly, his ego was in his corner, 100%. It shouted, "Don't sell, wait for it to come back, at least get out even!"

Then the market opened. He held his breath and stared at the quote. The opening price was $9.30, then $9.20, then $9.18, $9.14, and finally, $9.09. He felt sick. But even at that moment, he viewed each quote as validation that he was right. It would rebound. It had to.

Of course, it could go down to $9.00, that was support. But it couldn't go lower than that, because buyers will move in to support it. The volume was not as heavy as it should be if this was a real sell off. He shouldn't sell, this was actually a great time to buy.

New Trader watched as more of his money slipped away. $8.98 was the last quote. He was now down $185, and he was heading into the territory of the most he wanted to lose on any one trade. His lack of discipline, inability to stick to his trading plan, and his refusal to honor his trailing stop had cost him an additional $135.

He was sure there would be a bounce. It was at support and it was oversold. The buyers would have to scoop up the bargain. In a matter of seconds, SRRS made a move to $9.10, and then rolled over and plummeted to $8.80. The volume spiked half a day's volume and the stock fell fast with little price support.

He couldn't take it anymore. New Trader sold his stock.

He was demoralized. He felt like a failure for picking SRRS, and for not selling it when the stock opened below his planned stop. He had been admiring his profits for weeks, but in the end, he lost $275. He had wasted weeks on SRRS, pretending he was a big-time stock operator interpreting the chart, volume, and price. His emotions weighed heavily on him. He didn't want to talk to Rich Trader. He didn't want to trade. He felt like a loser.

How could he have believed that this trading thing would work?

After a few hours of brooding, he started to look at his streamer again. SRRS had gone to $8.49 and rallied back to a high of $8.97. But it was in a new range that morning, with the market pricing in the ending dominance of its specialty device.

Would it recover by earnings? No one knew. New Trader didn't care, he just wanted to make money. Now he understood that he could lose money on any trade, and that he could control what that amount was. He realized that if a stock met his exit price, trailing stop, or stop loss, the odds were that he was wrong about the trade. He should take that signal and get out.

It occurred to him that it was a lot like insurance. He didn't get mad paying for car insurance, even if he doesn't need it that month. But if he were to total his car, his insurance would protect him from financial ruin.

Stop losses and trailing stops protect traders from big losses when the trend never reverses. It keeps them from losing more money waiting for it to "come back." He was beginning to see how he could have locked in some gains if he could have stopped out during the regular market. Even if he was stopped out and then the stock reversed, he could buy it back, he reasoned.

He finally understood the importance of stop loss placement to avoid being stopped out unnecessarily. Additionally, the trailing stop would need to be carefully considered, to promote maximum gains while allowing the trend to run.

The great thing about this incident was that he learned it on his own, and he was lucky that it was with a small amount of money. His plan to buy a large position in 'out of the money' call options could have led to the loss of his entire account, or his full 1,000 share position could have cost him twice as much! Instead of losing $275, he would have lost $550.

He was analyzing his trades and thinking about what he had learned; he was thinking like a trader. He was learning the lessons that all successful traders must learn.

The books he read, Rich Trader's advice, and his own experiences were coming together.

He didn't feel like it at the time, but he was very fortunate.

"Good investing is a peculiar balance between the conviction to follow your ideas and the flexibility to recognize when you have made a mistake."

MICHAEL STEINHARDT

Rich Trader's Tip:

I don't think traders start making money until they mature and can see the big picture. We can easily become unrealistic and go down the wrong road; it's crucial that we stay on the road to success. If you need to ask others for their opinions about a trade, stop trading and develop a trading plan. It will take time to create your plan and test your strategies, but if you're not willing to put in the hours involved in learning to trade, you won't make it.

Recommended reading:

"Trading Habits" 39 of the World's Most Powerful Stock Market Rules" by Steve Burns & Holly Burns

TEN

New Traders give back profits by not having an exit strategy; Rich Traders lock in profits while they are there.

IT WAS his appointed day to visit Rich Trader, and soon New Trader was soon stepping onto his mentor's porch. A part of him was happy to receive another lesson, while the other part was mortified by his inability to follow his system. He could only imagine what the older trader would say. It was worth it, though. He knew his time was well spent with Rich Trader, and he hoped that any knowledge he gleaned would translate into cash.

He knocked lightly, and when Rich Trader opened the door, he was holding a steaming mug of coffee for both. New Trader took it with a smile of gratitude. He was struck by something he hadn't noticed about Rich Trader, previously; his poise.

He looked like the picture of success. Even relaxing around the house, he carried himself with a sense of purpose and intelligence, as though he planned every word and action. He always seemed refreshed and ready for the new day. New Trader knew he wanted to be like Rich Trader. He wanted the freedom, the confidence, and the security. That's why he traded.

"Thanks for the coffee."

"It's no trouble," Rich Trader said. "Come in."

New Trader followed him into the dining room.

"How's your trading been going?" Rich Trader looked at the younger man across from him. He seemed unusually tired.

"Well, every time I think I have it figured out, a curve ball hits me in the face," New Trader said, looking down into his cup.

Rich Trader chuckled.

"I know what you mean. I've taken similar hits right between the eyes. It's all part of your trading education. But you won't ever 'figure out' the market. You can't predict the markets; you can only react to the signals it gives you. At least, that's what I've learned so far."

"What would you suggest is the best way to lock in profits using a trading plan?"

"That depends on your trading plan, methodology, and system. Trend traders, like me, tend to take profits when trailing stops are hit. However, sometimes we have sell signals as a stock falls through a moving average support, or hits a new low for a certain number of days. We always let profits run as far as possible. We want to give the stock an opportunity to catch the big trends. A trend trader must capture large wins to pay for all the small losses."

Rich Trader took a sip of coffee before continuing.

"However, there are traders that trade support and resistance, and would sell their stock once it reaches the price they consider resistance. If your system is looking for short-term swings in price, like trading around an earnings announcement, you could have a target based on the historical price action of the stock."

"What do you mean by 'historical price action'?"

"I mean that if you're swing trading a stock and buying it a month before the underlying company announces its earnings, you would want to know how much the stock moved leading up into earnings announcements in the last year." Rich Trader cleared his throat.

"If the last four times the stock increased 8%, 7%, 10%, and 12%, in the four weeks prior to the announced earnings, it would be prudent to take profits when the stock was up in that range. You could also set a stop if it retraces to 7% when it's up 8% or more. If you're up 10% in this trade, the odds are that you already have all the profits you're going to get, and you need to look at taking them."

New Trader thought about this. "I didn't think about all those moving parts. I was just letting my profits run on my trade. Then an announcement demolished me in the pre-market. Then to make the matters worse, I didn't sell and take my original loss when it hit my trailing stop."

"You had bad luck, combined with an overextended profit, and failure to follow your trailing stops?"

"Yes," New Trader sighed, "all of the above."

"Well, that was a learning experience. That's also how plane crashes happen; it's never just one problem but a combination that results in catastrophe. It's usually bad weather, a new pilot's error, and a technical malfunction that results in a plane crash. There are too many safeguards in place for one thing to cause a catastrophic plane crash.

You should understand the stock you're trading, its volatility, daily price range, and historical movements leading into earnings. You should also understand how the earnings reports of similar companies affect your stock. Economic reports may also cause movement in your stock. Know it inside and out before you trade it.

You must focus on controlling your risk. When a stock moves against you and hits your stop or gaps down below your stop, get out. This is your insurance against ruin. Don't hope, don't try to predict, just sell. This will typically save you from further losses. After you sell, you can plan to get back in at a predetermined rally that fits your trading plan.

You must keep your ego out of the trade at all costs. Your goal is not to be right every time, your goal is to make money over the long-term. This is accomplished by your winners being bigger than your losers. Focus on being right big and wrong small."

New Trader scribbled notes in his notebook.

"When you decided not to sell your stock on the gap down, do you know which rules you were violating, psychology, risk, or methodology?"

New Trader frowned.

"I suppose I never thought of the psychology having a lot of rules before, but probably all of the above. My trading plan is based mainly on methodology. Do you have rules for the psychology of trading?"

"I have have some rules that have helped my trading over the past thirty years."

Rich Trader went to an old notebook next to his computer, flipped the cover open to the first page, and handed the handwritten page to New Trader:

- Read your trading rules and trading plan before trading every day.
- Never hope for a bounce back; cut losses at your predetermined stop loss or trailing stop price level.
- Always exercise discipline. Follow your predetermined trading plan.
- Don't overtrade.
- A successful trade is a trade that follows your trading plan and your system.
- Don't allow outside distractions during entries and exits; when you're trading, focus only on trading execution.
- Your opinion doesn't matter, only price action.
- Never try to predict. Follow trends, trend reversals, and your signals.
- Never fall into the trap of hindsight, instead focus on real-time trading.

✓ • Always respect the market and don't become arrogant.

"I learned most of these lessons the hard way by losing thousands of dollars. These are also in my trading journal." Rich Trader smiled.

"You know, a few months ago I would have thought this was just common sense, and that these rules didn't apply to me, but now I know better. I'm surprised at the difference between simulated trading and theory versus trading with real money. I haven't started my trading journal. I need to do that. I need to put all of your lessons into action."

Rich Trader nodded.

"To be successful in anything you have to learn from your mistakes and correct them. If you want to be a great golfer, going and hitting a bucket of balls with the wrong form every day won't make you better. You need to learn which club to use for different situations, how to hold the club properly, how to swing properly, and how hard to hit the ball depending on the distance you want the ball to travel.

Trading is no different. It's critical that you learn from your mistakes as quickly as possible and that you try not to repeat them. The market gives instant feedback about your performance, but you have to pay attention. Trading is very rewarding but it's not easy. It's a business like any other, and if you treat it like a business, you will do well."

They smiled at each other, and New Trader headed home with a notebook full of things to think about.

"Take your money off the table while it's still there. Trailing stops = keeping profits."

STEVE BURNS

Rich Trader's Tip:

In trading, the money isn't made on the entry, it's made on the exit. The art of the exit is critical to a trader's success. Profits can disappear if you don't take them at the right time, and small losses can become big losses if you don't cut them short. Alternatively, small profits can become large profits if you let them run until they stop moving in your favor. And finally, keeping capital tied up in a trade going nowhere can cause you to miss out on a good opportunity.

You must have a plan to get out of every trade before you get in. Before each trading day begins, think about what you will do based on where your trade is and where it may go. Exits are meant to minimize losses, and to lock in winning trades for maximum gains. An exit strategy is meant to allow your logical mind to make decisions on how to exit before your emotions get involved.

Recommended reading:

"Sell and Sell Short" by Alexander Elder

PART THREE
METHODOLOGY

ELEVEN

Most New Traders quit; Rich Traders persevere in the market until they are successful.

NEW TRADER HAD BEEN DOING MORE THINKING than trading, and once again, he wondered if trading was for him.

He loved trading and was desperate to be successful, but he decided he needed to spend more time studying. He searched online and found popular trading books, and sites that provided free stock charts. He read the words of wise traders and studied the charts to better understand price action.

He worked at developing historically successful trading systems. He back tested them, and then forward tested them with very small position sizes to develop an accurate record.

Now he understood what it would cost to become a successful

trader; study, experience, and perseverance. He was ready to pay the price.

New Trader had a weekend off and he was ready to study. He had a stack of trading books next to his reading chair, several financial magazines, his favorite financial newspapers, and plans to visit a few sites online.

After a healthy breakfast and some caffeine, he was ready. He flipped his journal to a blank page and prepared to take notes.

After studying many charts, he began to see trends; stocks move up or down, they move slow or fast, and they may have a tight price range or a loose price range, but most stocks trend over the long-term.

Moving averages also seemed to play a part in price ranges. He could see what looked like prices literally bouncing off these lines. They had a magical, yet predictable quality to them.

The 10-day, 21-day, and 50-day moving averages seemed to be the ones that affected stock prices the most. When he expanded his charts for long time frames and looked at the price action of stock indexes like the S&P 500, Dow Jones Industrial Average, and NASDAQ, it looked like the 100-day and 200-day moving averages also came into play as lines of support or resistance. It seemed that if a stock or index broke these lines, it was hard to get back over them or under them, possibly signaling a change in the trend. It was fascinating. Stocks of smaller companies seemed to move faster than larger companies. He also noticed large companies were more likely to be range-bound than smaller ones.

He spent four hours that morning examining chart after chart, and as he did, he was amazed at all the patterns that he noticed for the first time.

Bollinger Bands caught his eye, because most of the time it appeared when a stock price would scrape against the top of the bands in an uptrend, and the bottom of the bands in a downtrend. He looked at the different technical indicators: Moving Averages, Bollinger Bands, MACD, and RSI.

He decided to take a short break when his stomach reminded

him, loudly, that it was lunch time. Three slices of re-heated pizza and he was ready for more research.

He stumbled upon chart patterns on a respected trader's web site and studied each pattern. He reviewed a cup with handles, ascending triangles, head and shoulders, flags and pennants, descending triangles, and wedge formations. He read theories about trader psychology, which were said to cause these patterns to form. He wondered how often they worked, and if they could be incorporated into a winning system. He thought he may be able to use these patterns to be a technical trader, he just needed to find his comfort zone.

He was searching for a technique he could trade successfully and faithfully. He needed a plan with a high winning percentage because he hated losing trades. He wanted to trade a system with a 60%-win rate, and he wanted his average win to be twice the size of his average loss; a 2:1 ratio. He knew what he wanted, now he had to find it.

So far, hot stocks in uptrends appealed to him the most. He liked the idea of trading stocks that everyone wanted. He liked trades that were based on a company's business fundamentals, and he liked the market being bullish on his pick.

He reviewed his notes and was pleased with himself. He had learned that while fundamentals and earnings expectations could tell him *what* to buy, he needed charts and technical indicators to tell him *when* to buy.

The correct buy signals seemed to be on a pullback to support, or a high-volume breakout to new highs. In the hot stocks he was eyeing, the pullback was usually at the 10-day moving average. However, some of the rocket stocks had gone through the roof and never experienced a pullback. Did he have the guts to trade these breakouts? He needed rules, and he needed to follow what he decided were the highest probability trades.

That afternoon, he began reading the stack of trading books. He read the covers, the table of contents, and the author bios. He started reading a chapter or two of each book. By the time evening arrived, he had chosen his five favorite books and continued to read until midnight. The principles of trend trading, money management, and chart reading struck a chord with New Trader. He decided to be a trend trader, looking to profit on trends.

He would use charts to pick his buy and sell point, and after everything he had learned and experienced, he knew his opinion didn't matter. What did matter were the prices buyers were willing to pay for a stock, and the price sellers were asking for their stock.

Price was reality and personal opinions had no value.

He started to view the stock market as a democracy with the volume representing the number of votes cast in a direction. Stock prices weren't based on a company's underlying valuation. Instead, prices were a composite of all traders' opinions about the future expectations of making money on the stock. Could fear and greed drive prices more than a company's value? This thought was interesting to him, because he had never thought about what drove price.

His head was spinning with thoughts about the markets. He fell asleep in his reading chair with a book in hand. He hardly noticed his stiff muscles when he awoke the next morning, still in his chair. He was excited about everything he was learning. He picked up where he had left off. He read all day, only stopping when he had to. He was a man on a mission, and as he went, he jotted down key lessons on growth investing.

Trade stocks with double-digit earnings increases year over year.

The general market direction determines the direction of your stock.

Only trade the leaders in the hottest industries.

To guarantee they are liquid, pick stocks that trade at least a million shares per day.

Look for stocks that are close to all-time highs and have great support.

Stocks that have new products with heavy consumer demand, or a new business model with an edge in an industry, should have the highest earnings expectations.

Stay away from illiquid penny stocks; trade stocks on the major exchanges.

Cut losses on a stock's price at predetermined amounts, 7%-10% maximum, with a position size of 10%-20% of total trading capital.

Never invest in a stock that is in the beginning of a downtrend.

Never bet against a government taking corrective action in the economy.

Some of this he had learned from Rich Trader, but he picked up many details he hadn't thought about before. He was more than halfway through several good books on trader psychology. By now he knew that having the right mindset would be critical to his trading success. He jotted down these lessons:

You must decide that you will trade until you're successful. Quitters give up when they are tired and frustrated. Winners don't quit until they have won.

To win at trading, you must think and act like a winner, not a whiner.

A trading system's success is directly influenced by a trader's discipline.

Listen and learn, but also verify the source and whether what is being taught will work in real-time.

Don't start trading real money until you have done due diligence on your system.

Never trade without a written trading plan.

Reduce your risk of ruin still making an acceptable profit.

Your system should show your equity curve growing in back tests or paper trading over the course of a year.

Have an accountability partner whom you can talk to about your trading.

Keep a trading journal with as much detail as possible. Include how you feel and what you're thinking about each trade.

New Trader was surprised at the similarities between what he had experienced in his own trading, and what the books had to say about the psychology of trading. Many of these notes reinforced what

Rich Trader had been teaching him. He would continue to read into the night, committed to persevering until he was successful in trading.

"The harder you work, the harder it's to surrender."

VINCE LOMBARDI

Rich Trader's Tip:

New traders will be tempted to give up, particularly when they see that the first few years are more about studying and learning rather than making money. But there are some compelling reasons not to give up on trading; it will teach you about yourself, it will make you better in other aspects of your life, it can create a consistent stream of income, and nothing else offers the same level of control over your personal finances or your future.

Recommended reading:

"Trading for a Living" by Alexander Elder

TWELVE

ι

New Traders hop from system to system the moment they suffer a loss; Rich Traders stick with a winning system even when it's losing.

NEW TRADER WAS LEARNING from various sources, a mentor who has been successfully trading full-time for many years, books by other successful traders, and studying charts to better understand repeating patterns. And on Monday morning, he decided he would like to spend some more time with his mentor.

He loved that he had an accountability partner in Rich Trader with whom he could share his ideas, and keep himself on track. He was dedicated to using a trading journal to learn about himself and his system as he traded, and he was determined to not repeat his mistakes.

He knocked on Rich Trader's door, and he answered almost immediately and ushered New Trader inside.

As soon as they were settled in his mentor's house, New Trader blurted out: "Do you still trade, or did you retire?"

"I still trade, but I use a less aggressive approach," Rich Trader answered.

"What does that mean?"

"I currently utilize a trend trading system using stock indexes. This system is only adjusted in the first or last hour of trading each day, and only if I get a signal."

"I've always pictured successful traders glued to their computer screens all day, buying and selling, sweating and stressing, watching every news development."

"This is just my personal system right now, and it fits my personality and my temperament. There are also day traders and swing traders who actively trade all day and make money doing so. In my opinion, trend trading has proven to be the most effective way to trade, but you can make money in many ways, if you follow the rules.

Disciplined traders can make money trading any system with an edge, but traders without discipline can't make money trading any system, because they're unlikely to follow it. They'll try to judge signals instead of following them. They'll try to predict the market instead of following what the price and volume are telling them. The sad thing is, after they take a few losses, they give up. This is unfortunate, because one of the next few trades could be the big winner that pays for all the small losses. The beauty of my current system is that it's simple, and when it catches a trend, it makes large gains without making many adjustments."

"You recommend trend trading, then?" New Trader asked anxiously.

"I recommend following the principles we've discussed, and trading the style that fits your personality. What are you comfortable trading? Do you want to sit in front of your computer all day and try to scalp small moves in big positions? Do you want to trade the index and follow the current trend using technical signals like moving averages? Do Bollinger Bands appeal to you?

You can also be a growth investor, buying the hottest stocks in the market with the greatest earnings expectations, using charts to know when to buy and when to sell. It's like any other career, you will be successful doing what you're passionate about."

"I just want to do what makes the most money."

"The system you follow with discipline over time, that you have faith in, is the one that will make you the most money." Rich Trader smiled confidently.

"What do you mean? The system that I am best suited for will be the one that is most profitable for me? Why do you think I can't follow any type of system that has the best returns?"

"Some people are natural bargain shoppers; it goes against their nature to buy a stock or index at an all-time high. They would probably do better to wait for a pullback to a moving average support or the bottom of a Bollinger band. They can still make money with something on their watchlist getting a pullback in an uptrend.

Another trader may be aggressive and feel good about buying the breakout because it means his stock has buyers who are bullish. This trader is likely to buy a monster stock on his watchlist that doesn't pullback before a large, profitable run. Both traders will be successful in the long run, because both are using systems that work. However, it would make the aggressive trader uneasy to wait for a pullback that may not happen, and the bargain buyer would feel sick for paying all-time highs for a stock, no matter how it performed over the next few days. They will both be uncomfortable with their trades, which will in turn probably render them unsuccessful in the end. The aggressive trader will lose his patience and buy a stock that has already run too far, and the bargain hunter will panic and sell stock he deems too expensive at the first sign of weakness."

"Could you sum up success in trading, then?"

"Hmm..." Rich Trader scratched his chin.

"Well, let's see. Find a style of trading you're interested in and feels right to you, and learn everything you can about that style. Develop a system that is historically profitable. Develop a watchlist of stocks and/or exchange traded funds that have the characteristics that will make them good candidates for your system, and test it on paper over a few months through different market cycles to see how it performs. If you're convinced it's a winning system, begin trading it with small positions; just enough to be profitable and cover commission costs. Slowly increase your position size as you start to understand all the moving parts in your specific system. Journal your thoughts and feelings as you trade so you can learn what causes you to over-trade/under-trade, or not follow your system. Continue to learn and grow by reading books written by successful traders, and continue to network with seasoned traders and politely ask for their advice and support."

New Trader realized that these weren't just opinions, but what he had learned that had made him a millionaire a few times over.

Rich Trader continued.

"As a new trader, you're like a medical intern, sampling all the fields of medicine to see what fits. You should spend some time day trading, swing trading, position trading, trading growth stocks, and trend trading. You should develop a watchlist of fast and slow movers; it should include big and small cap index ETFs and leveraged ETFs. You should follow your interests and experiment on paper and in small positions. Listen to your emotions as you trade. Your stress may be telling you that a volatile stock moves too fast for you to handle. Your boredom may be telling you that the system you're trading is not giving you enough of a return to make it worth your time. Your uncertainty in a trade may be telling you that you have not looked at the historical performance sufficiently enough to have faith in it."

"So, I'm looking for my system, and not just a system that makes money?"

"If your trading system doesn't fit your tolerance for risk and reward, and you can't develop faith in its performance, then the odds are against your success. You can measure the success of your system with these."

He pulled out a blank work sheet and explained each line to New Trader.

- The winning percentage: wins divided by total trades
- Pay off ratio: Profits versus losses
- Your largest winning trade
- Your largest losing trade
- Average winning trade
- Average losing trade
- Largest percentage drawdown: The most money you have lost in a row divided by your starting capital before the drawdown
- Average percentage drawdown: What is the average money lost during your losing streaks divided by your account before each loss, then divided by number of total losses?
- Largest numbers of straight losses
- Largest numbers of straight wins
- Total percentage profit for different time periods

These records will build faith in your system. After 100 trades, you should begin to see patterns of how your system performs in different market environments. You may also see flaws which you can adjust to make it perform better, such as a wider trailing stop or how it works best on specific stocks or indexes, et cetera. The point is to continually work toward building a trading system that matches your beliefs about the market, which has an advantage you can verify, risks you can control, and a system in which you can develop faith and have the tenacity to follow long-term."

"Everyone has a game plan until they get punched in the mouth."

MIKE TYSON

Rich Trader's Tip:

Here is my personal trading methodology:

- I like trading systems with limited screen time. I prefer to make trading decisions in the first and last hour of the trading day and not waste time glued to the screen.
- I prefer using a system with end of day signals for entries instead of day trading. Often, the best exits to lock in profits are at the open. That frees up about 30 hours a week for back tests, chart studies, reading, and enjoying life.
- I like systems that trade above the level of random price noise and look at the bigger picture and long-term trend.
- I prefer to trade price action rather than attempting to make sense out of the financial headlines or the opinions of others.
- I prefer simplicity over complexity. I have been profitable over the years using only moving averages, RSI, and price action to capture trends.
- I like to limit risk exposure with only 10%-20% position sizes in most stocks and leveraged trading vehicles at one time to limit risk of large drawdowns. I will take a bigger position in a diversified index.
- My favorite signals are oversold price levels extended far from the 10-day EMA and/or near the 30 RSI for reversion to the mean trades. I like breakouts of price

bases to all-time highs, and a moving average crossover system with the 10-day crossing over the 50-day moving average as powerful trend trades.

- I don't have a portfolio of stocks, I have trades and trading systems.

Recommended reading:

"How to Make Money in Stocks" by William O'Neal

THIRTEEN

New Traders place trades based on opinions; Rich Traders place trades based on probabilities.

RICH TRADER HAD INVITED him to go to dinner, and New Trader was buzzing with excitement. This was a first, and he felt he was becoming closer friends with his mentor, maybe even a peer. He had a lot of respect for the older man, and their growing friendship meant a lot to him.

Not wanting to appear rude, he decided not to take notes over dinner. He hoped he could remember it all later. While he was getting ready, he walked over and looked at his pile of notes. He noticed that they seemed to be grouped into one of three categories: methodology, risk management, or psychology. He now understood that having an issue in any one of these areas would cause him to fail.

Even if his trading method had a large winning percentage, if he didn't control his risk, he would eventually lose the capital in his account. On the other hand, he could cut his losses like a professional every time, but if he didn't have a method that was profitable historically, or in the current market environment, he wouldn't be successful in the long-term. If his system didn't have a strong winning edge over the market, his repetitive losses, combined with commission costs, would whittle down his account until it was too small to trade effectively. And even with a winning method and risk control, he had to maintain self-control and discipline.

Trading was turning out to be harder than he expected. There was much more to it than buying stocks which were going upward. There is no free money; profit must be earned through homework, discipline, courage, patience, and perseverance in the market.

These were lessons he was learning through dabbling in trading, reading stories of trading legends, and spending time with his mentor. He was also studying charts and paper trading systems he was testing.

He arrived at one of Rich Trader's favorite restaurants that evening. Rich Trader was seated at a large table in the corner. New Trader smiled and walked across the bustling room. There was already a bottle of wine on the table.

"Hello, New Trader. Please sit down. Order whatever you'd like; my treat." New Trader thought this was very generous and looked over the menu carefully while Rich Trader poured him a glass of wine.

When the waiter arrived, New Trader was the first to order.

"I'd like the New York strip."

"And how would you like that cooked?"

He had to think for a moment.

"Well done," he finally responded.

"And I'd like the porterhouse, medium-rare," Rich Trader added.

As the waiter left, Rich Trader sensed New Trader's uneasiness.

"You seem uncomfortable."

"Sorry, I can't help but think about how much this is going to cost." New Trader said while nervously folding his napkin.

"You're worried how much this is going to cost me? You must stop thinking of money in those terms. You're probably calculating how many hours you would have to work to earn enough money to pay for this meal."

"Yes. I'm always looking to save money, not spend it."

"While I agree that you should spend money wisely, and frugality is a great way to get your first trading account, I also believe it's important to enjoy the money you have earned, and spend it on the things you think are important. While I couldn't care less about a new car or bigger house, I do like to spend my money on traveling and dining with friends. When you spend money, you need to ask yourself if you're getting the value for the money that you're spending. If you are, then you should relax and enjoy it. If not, then don't spend your money in that way again. Please relax, these are trading profits well spent," said Rich Trader with a grin.

"Your early years will be challenging, and it will take time for you to understand my perspective. Like we've talked about in the past, you must understand that in your early trading career, your losses are the tuition you pay to learn how to trade. It's no different than college tuition you would pay to learn any career. When you have advanced as a trader and have worked out your system, the losing trades are your cost of doing business; they will be paid for by your winning trades."

"When I lose, I feel like a failure, like I don't know what I'm doing." New Trader said.

"If you follow your trading plan 100% from start to finish, then it's a successful trade. If you make a mistake but learned a lesson from the trade, it was money well spent to improve your skills. Mistakes that lose real money tend to be remembered and corrected more than money lost in paper trading or simulators."

"What is the best way to deal with my stress when I'm losing money? It still makes me sick to lose money." New Trader asked with a frown.

"You have to look at dollars as points while you're trading. Professionals don't count their profits or losses while they are working. A surgeon doesn't count how much they are making during a surgery. 'Great, I made an incision, I just made $400. I'm removing the gall stone, that's another $800.' That's not how professionals think about their work. They focus on the correct technique and the profits come because of their hard work and diligence. Don't count your wins as they happen, because if you lose them it will hurt even more. Focus instead on following your system, taking your signals as you get them, and the profits will follow."

"How do I increase my chance of success using my system?"

"I'll give you a few tips that may increase your chance of success.

First, you need to trade with the market trend. You have better odds if you're trading long in an uptrend and shorting in a downtrend. The best way to determine this is to look at a chart of the S&P 500 or NASDAQ; if price is above the 200-day moving average line, then you should be trading long in the uptrend. If the price is below the 200-day moving average, you're in a downtrend. If the market is in an uptrend, then you can go long based on your predetermined parameters. But you will lower your chance of success substantially by trying to trade long when the market is going down. When a torpedo hits a ship, the whole ship sinks, not just part of it."

"What you're saying is that I trade in sync with the overall market in whatever direction it's currently in?"

"That's step one...

You need to buy at the sweet spot on the chart for the stock or index. These are high consolidation areas where there is volume and a crossroad for decision. They include a breakout to a new all-time high, where everyone has made money and have little interest in selling. A breakout could also be in a long-term resistance point, like a 10-day, 20-day, or 50-day moving average, which a price finally rises above.

On the flip side, if you're shorting a growth stock and the price goes under the 50-day moving average, that's likely the place to look at going short, because it indicates that it doesn't have buyers to support its price in the downtrend.

Sweet spots are also at a point of support on a chart in an uptrend; this could be the bottom of a Bollinger band which has held for a couple of months. The support could be at a specific moving average like the 10-day or 20-day moving average, or an actual price level. It depends on the specific chart and your ability to see the repeating pattern. It's important to buy at that point after you have identified it through studying the chart. Don't hesitate, buy it when your signal says to because you don't want to wait and chase it after the fact. If you buy too early or wait and buy too late, you lower the probability of success."

"I need to take my signals, overcome fear, not be trigger-shy, and not be greedy and buy too soon. Got it," said New Trader, getting the feeling that Rich Trader had told him this previously.

Rich Trader continued.

"Don't trade based on your opinions or feelings, only trade your system. Don't trade your system until you have back tested it using software and studied past charts, so you have a good idea of the win ratio and risk-versus-reward payout ratio. You will need at least 50 to 100 hypothetical trades over multiple types of market environments for an accurate back test. You also need to forward test it on paper or in a simulator to see how it performs in the current market, and how well you trade it. Then, and only then, you're ready to trade. In the stock market, opinions and feelings are wrong most of the time, but the current trend is right much of the time. You have a good chance of being right over the long-term when you follow a proven system with discipline.

Becoming an expert in specific stocks and in your chosen method puts you at an advantage. If you want to be a day trader, you need to understand how stocks trade during each hour increment of the day, when the most volume is traded, and when the market is most likely to trend. Your trading should be based on these observations. You might choose to sit out the first hour because it's too choppy. Your system might be to buy breakouts after 10 a.m. on your watchlist, or buy off a bounce in support after noon. Your system might have you trade long while the major indexes are green, or short when they are red. Or your trade direction might be based on the weekly time frame if they were above the 10-day moving average.

As an expert day trader, you would build a watchlist of stocks which had price action that fit your trading system. If you were going to play daily trends or breakouts, you would need volatile stocks with large daily average price ranges. You would build watchlists of stocks based on these characteristics and become an expert on how they traded; their trends, average volume, and the percent and dollar amount they moved each day. You should know exactly when they had upcoming earnings announcements, or anything else that may affect their price. You should change this list when you find better candidates than the ones you were trading. Someone who has studied something for hundreds if not thousands of hours will almost always beat someone with just a passing interest. There is an undeniable advantage to those who know what they are doing. In the stock market, money flows from those who don't know how to trade to those who do.

Follow the volume, smart money knows where the action and profits are and it's up to you to find them. Monster stocks are not hidden under a rock, they're generally household names, even before they go up an additional 200% to 500%. When a company has wild earnings expectations, traders and investors know about it. The price rises along with the volume. This can be found on the highest volume traded list on major web sites and in business newspapers.

Day traders increase the volumes of stocks which are perfect for day trading. Option writers write options on equities which have movement that they can trade options on. Maximum volume flows into stocks and Exchange Traded Funds, which have the greatest potential for successful trading. Trade these equities. Don't fall into the trap of hearing about a hot pick from unreliable sources. Many of these sources are pumpers trying to get people to buy so they can sell what they already hold. Stay in the high stocks where the volume is. This will close the bid/ask spread so you don't lose money when you buy and sell, and you will always have a buyer ready to buy at the current bid price."

"To summarize, to have a high probability of success in my trading I should:

- Trade only in the direction of the overall market trend.
- Let my system make all the trading decisions, not my opinions and feelings.
- Buy only at the sweet spot on a chart.
- Become an expert in the method and the stocks I trade on my watchlist.
- Trade where the volume is, not in illiquid stocks or markets."

New Trader looked up from his scribble-covered napkin. "Right?"

"That's how we win," responded Rich Trader as their food arrived.

"This puts the odds on my side." New Trader mumbled to himself. "Oh, can I have another napkin?" Their waiter smiled and quickly left the table.

"These five dynamics working together can help put you in the 10% of traders who make money consistently over time."

The waiter returned with a pile of new napkins, and New Trader smiled in gratitude. He was pretty sure he was going to need a few more to get through this night. He should have brought his notebook.

"Well, that's where I want to be, so that's just what I'll have to do."

"In the stock market and in Las Vegas, you make money on the difference between playing the true odds and the opponent's disregard of the odds."

HARVEY FRIEDENTAG

Rich Trader's Tip:

Only price pays. In trading, emotions and egos are expensive collaborators. Our goal as traders is to capture price moves inside our time frame, while limiting our drawdowns in capital. The longer I have traded, the more I have become an advocate of price action. Moving away from the perils of opinions and predictions has improved my mental well-being and my bottom line.

Relying on facts and price data, rather than being tossed around by your own subjective feelings, will insure your long-term profitability.

Recommended reading:

"High Probability Trading" by Marcel Link

FOURTEEN

New Traders try to predict; Rich Traders follow what the market is telling them.

"WHAT DO you think the market will do today?"

"I have no idea."

"Which stocks do you like?"

"The ones that go up."

"Are you long or short in the market?"

"My system has me long."

"Do you think this uptrend will continue...?"

"I have no idea."

Rich Trader gritted his teeth.

"Do you think the job report coming out this morning will be good or bad?" New Trader asked, yet another attempt to get an opinion from his mentor.

"I don't know if a good report will cause the uptrend to continue or if it will have traders selling the news. I don't predict, I don't have an opinion, and I really don't know. What I do know is that following trends makes me money, and my system captures the profits in trends and gets me out when it reverses."

"I'm still trying to wrap my brain around how a trader who doesn't predict prices makes money. Isn't predicting where prices are going the only way to make money?"

"First of all, that's impossible, the future hasn't happened yet, so how can it be predicted? Money is made by being right on the direction of your trade. The direction of the market or a stock generally stays in one overall trend with few changes. A stock, or the market, is usually in the process of making either a higher high price along with higher low prices over the short term, or lower high prices and lower low prices. This can usually be measured over any time frame by checking the chart. This doesn't predict, it shows you the trend. You have better odds by going with the trend than trying to predict anything."

"You're saying you read the market, you don't try to predict it?"

"Exactly. I read charts, I trade patterns, and I react to changes in trends. Most importantly, I follow the market. It tells me what to do. There is no way one person can predict what all market participants are going to do, and relate that to all the moving parts of the economy, world politics, and monetary policy. And that's not counting random events. It's absurd to think that someone's successful prediction is more than just luck.

Think about it this way, when someone makes a big prediction before an event, they have a 50% chance of being correct, and with everyone weighing in, it can look like there's something at play other than luck. And when someone is right about a trend, people rarely check their track record to see how often they were mistaken in the past. They become a guru until the next few predictions don't come true, and people move on to the next person who is right on a big call."

"Okay, you don't believe in psychics and prophets in the stock market. I get it," said New Trader with a wide smile.

"What I do believe, is that traders can make money by consistently following the market's direction. The point of creating your trading system is to develop signals that tell you when a trend begins and when it ends. The signals you use to determine a trend are price and volume. All other technical indicators are derivatives of these two.

You can make a system as complex as you would like, but I have seen people make millions and never use complicated technical indicators. Many of the new, complex indicators were invented in modern times with the help of computers, and few legendary traders of the last 100 years used them. The tools I work with are price, volume, candlestick charts, and moving averages for trends, sometimes looking for overextended price trends using the RSI. That is just my personal choice; you should use any tool that helps you make money. Just be sure to limit your indicators to a manageable level so you don't confuse yourself. Three or four are usually plenty for most traders."

"Just to be clear, the purpose of the system I am building is to catch trends and to find common variables in the past that are identified at the beginning or end of a trend?" New Trader asked.

"The price and volume of a stock reveal investor and trader behavior; human behavior never changes. It creates patterns you can observe. Greed and fear come into play, and carry trends far beyond where rational, fundamental valuations could take them. The market is going to go where the votes carry it; your job is to vote with the majority."

"Trade What's Happening...Not What You Think Is Gonna Happen."

DOUG GREGORY

Rich Trader's Tip:

If someone thinks they can predict things often enough to create an edge, it's the height of arrogance or ignorance. The only thing we can do with any certainty is to follow price action wherever it leads. We can learn how the market acts by studying historical data, chart patterns, and trends. We can study how human greed, fear, and ego affect price movements and use that knowledge to our advantage.

Recommended reading:

"You Can Still Make It in the Market" by Nicolas Darvas

FIFTEEN

New Traders trade against the trend; Rich Traders follow the markets trend.

A market trend is a perceived tendency of financial markets to move in a direction over time. These trends are classified as secular for long time frames, primary for medium time frames, and secondary for short time frames. Traders attempt to identify market trends using technical analysis, a framework which characterizes market trends as predictable price tendencies within the market when price reaches support and resistance levels, varying over time. -Wikipedia

NEW TRADER READ through the definition several times and contemplated its meaning.

"The general course or prevailing tendency" made sense to him. Most investors acquire stock and hold it for increased profits, or they sell stocks because they are losing money and fears they could lose more.

Markets, stocks, and sectors all have price patterns and a prevailing tendency in one direction or the other over different time frames. When studying charts, he saw more trends over the long-term, and more range-bound charts in the short-term.

It looked like most stock charts moved inside price bases for weeks or months before making a run for a short-term high or low in price. Each stock was typically closer to the 52-week high or low, and rarely in the middle. The best performing stocks were near all-time highs in price, while the worst were making all-time lows.

He could now identify uptrends as stocks with a current price above a 50-day moving average, and downtrends in stocks because the current price was under the 200-day moving average. It was also obvious to him that when the market was in an uptrend, most stocks were in an uptrend.

He had learned that there were stocks which were leaders and had the strongest uptrends, and other stocks which lagged in their own downtrends, regardless of how strong the uptrend was in the general market. The best performing stocks had the highest earnings expectations, while the laggards had failing earnings because of lost market share or antiquated business models. Investment money flows to the stocks that have the highest earnings expectations.

It was time for what was becoming his daily dose of Rich Trader. He wanted to ask about the older man's experience trading trends.

New Trader and Rich Trader agreed to meet at a lake halfway between their houses. New Trader showed up just as the sun rose about the tree line. He felt the warmth on his skin as he waited comfortably on a bench facing the lake. Rich Trader approached moments later, and smiled when he saw that they both brought a loaf of bread to feed the ducks.

Rich Trader sat down on the bench and opened his bag. "I've always thought that bringing them bread was the best defense. A few of them are pretty pushy."

After several minutes of bread tossing, the young trader started with the question that had caused him the most confusion, "What are the best ways to identify and trade trends?"

"That's a good question. You search for increasing volume; you look for the highest volume stocks and ETFs, and look for new high and new low prices. Ideally, you would like to find a stock that has been in a tight price range for a few months. For example, a stock with a low of $95 and a high of $100 that suddenly breaks to a new all-time high of $101, on twice the average daily volume. That is a trend right from the start. Sellers are no longer willing to give up their stock at $100, and buyers are willing to pay $101 because they think it will go up and they will make money.

Trend traders don't care why it's going up, they only care that it's happening. Trend traders are not bullish or bearish; they don't care which direction the market is moving, only that it's moving. The trend trader's system would have been just as likely to sell the same stock short at $94 as he would have been to go long at $101. Many trend traders have become millionaires following simple systems that use price as the trigger to buy and sell. They have capitalized on trading stocks and commodities that are trending."

Rich Trader had been tossing bread while he talked. The ducks seemed hungrier than usual today, and that was saying something.

"And what causes trends?"

"In short, supply and demand for the stock. New buyers drive up the price, or the company's product or service is in demand which pushes up earnings, and that brings in more buyers hoping to profit from the fundamentals.

Emotions like greed and fear can cause equities to overshoot fundamental valuations by absurd amounts. In a downtrend, fear increases with each tick downward in price, and the investors who have lost money throw in the towel to avoid large losses. At the same time, some traders short the stock in anticipation of making money on the fall. Downtrends feed on losses because buyers have a difficult time buying when they only see other traders losing money."

Rich Trader took a deep breath and continued.

"Uptrends can escalate quickly, because greed pushes more buyers to jump onboard as a stock rockets upward. Fearful of losing out on a large uptrend, traders wait for a pullback, or give up and just buy it at a high price. Others who sold the stock short have to cover by buying it back, adding more buying pressure to the uptrend."

New Trader was listening, but he was also studying the ducks. They were greedy creatures. The more bread they ate, the more they wanted.

"A trend trader only needs to catch a large piece of the price movement inside a trend to make money. A counter trend trader has the odds stacked against them because they have to pick a big reversal on the top or bottom to be successful."

"Do I have to buy new highs as a trend trader?" New Trader was now paying close attention to his companion.

"No, not at all. If you can establish that the stocks on your watchlist are in an uptrend, you can also buy on pullbacks to create better risk/reward ratios. You can measure pullbacks by looking at charts for support. Your stock may have support at the 10-day moving average or the 20-day moving average over the last two months. If you can verify that the price found support at the 20-day moving average and then went back up, your system can consist of buying at the 20-day moving average inside a longer uptrend.

Then you must decide when you want to sell. Depending on the strength of the trend, you can let it ride if it doesn't lose the 20-day again, or you can sell when it reaches the top of a Bollinger Band, or when it starts reading as overbought on an oscillator like the RSI. It depends on that stock's chart. In a strong uptrend, the 10-day and 20-day moving averages may not be touched by the price for weeks.

The moving average will trend higher in uptrends, so if you're using only the moving average as your signal, you will make a profit when your stop is triggered because the price at which you sell is much larger than your buy price. You may also have a stock that bounces around in a slow uptrend inside a range, with a low of $95 and a high of $100 for weeks. It could make higher highs and higher lows, like a new low of only $96 and a new high of $101. Instead of breaking to new highs, it slowly goes higher by increasing the high and low price levels of the trading range. In this instance, moving averages work best by filtering the prices of the trend.

Additionally, price moving above the long-term moving averages like the 200-day and 250-day can be used to signal the beginning of a new uptrend breaking out of a downtrend. These systems create some of the best risk/reward ratios. They are used to signal the end of a downtrend or bear market, and the potential for a new uptrend or bull market."

"So, what you're saying is that a system can buy off different signals in an uptrend, not only a new high, and I want to take signals that make me long in a bull market and short in a bear market."

"Exactly. A good way to lose money is to go short in a bull market or long in a bear market; the probabilities are stacked against you. It's arrogant to think you can call tops, bottoms, and market reversals based on predictions. All decisions must be based on quantified signals that show the potential of capturing a trend. The only thing traders should attempt to do is measure the direction of the market, how to trade it effectively, and where to cut their losses when it reverses."

"What percentage of the time do trend traders win?" asked New Trader, expecting a high percentage.

"The best trend traders' wins are between 40% and 60%. They are successful because they win big and they lose small. The drawback is that they can lose many times in a row during choppy market conditions. However, over the long-term their wins compound and their equity can grow to impressive amounts. Your profitability isn't determined by the percentage of wins as much as the size of your wins and losses."

"Sounds like you speak from personal experience," said New Trader.

"Yes, I do. Like many others, I have benefited from trend trading over a long period of time. The hardest part may be to keep faith in your system when it suffers several losses in a row. It also gets more challenging as your capital grows larger. For most people, a $100,000 trade feels different than a $10,000."

"I wish I had that problem," New Trader chuckled.

"I trade a system that is purely technical, and it's based on past performance. My system only depends on the trend itself, not my opinions or news stories. I don't trade off fundamental valuations or earnings expectations; I trade based on other trader's participation in the markets as is illustrated through their buying and selling. I don't predict the trend, I follow the trend. I measure the trend through volume, price, and moving averages.

Trading *is* rocket science – you find a rocket and ride it."

"There is only one side to the stock market, not the bull side or the bear side, but the right side. It took me longer to get that general principle fixed firmly in my mind than it did most of the more technical phases of the game of stock market speculation."

JESSE LIVERMORE

Rich Trader's Tip:

Quantified trading signals can be based on different, yet equally profitable strategies. Momentum signals are based on buying strength. Momentum traders wait for a strong move in a stock, and then buy and hold a position for a short time if it continues to move in their favor. Breakout signals are based on buying all-time highs, 52-week highs, or prices moving through resistance and trying to buy high and sell higher. Breakouts are bought to catch a strong and fast-moving stock. Buying a long-term price support level or an oversold oscillator like the 30 RSI, attempts to create a good risk/reward ratio based on buying a deep dip in a market or stock that is in historical uptrend. Finally, trend following signals attempt to move in the direction of the long-term trend by the path of least resistance.

Recommended reading:

"*Trend Following*" by Michael Covel

SIXTEEN

New Traders follow their emotions, which put them at a disadvantage; Rich Traders follow systems that give them an advantage.

OVER THE NEXT MONTH, New Trader diligently studied charts, stocks and their behavior, and perfected his system for choosing the best stocks. He created a list of the characteristics that he was looking for:

- They were within 5% of all-time highs in price.
- They each traded over five million shares a day, some much more.
- They all had new products or business models that gave them an edge over their competition, and they were all influencing their industry and/or consumer behavior.

- Each of them had earnings increases and/or sales increases of over 20% year over year for the same quarter, some much more.
- All the companies were expected to continue to grow in sales and profits, and take over or change the marketplace.

This was the foundation of his trading plan, and using it to guide him, he created a watchlist with five stocks that he thought were leaders in the market. All his stocks were in established uptrends, with prices above all key moving averages like the 10-day, 20-day, and 50-day.

None of the stocks had lost their 50-day moving averages in the past six weeks. They typically stayed above the 20-day moving average, touching it only in market retracements. These stocks spent over 80% of their time above the 10-day moving average, going to new high prices right around the last two earnings announcements.

New Trader set up Bollinger Bands on his charts with the setting of a 20-day moving average and two standard deviations. These stocks' prices spent most of their time along the top of their Bollinger Bands. He noticed that many of the stocks in downtrends had their price across the bottom of the Bollinger Bands, and these downtrending stocks were almost the reverse of his watchlist. On those charts, the 10-day moving average was below the 20-day moving average, which was also below the 50-day moving average. The stocks that had really crashed were also below their 200-day moving average.

He was determined that his system would capture uptrends in the strongest stocks. From his analysis, it looked like the 10-day moving average was a good support in uptrends and resistance in downtrends. I also looked like the top Bollinger Band was resistance in uptrends and the bottom band was support in downtrends. This wasn't always the case, but it was true most of the time.

HE STUDIED stock charts in uptrends:

Courtesy of StockCharts.com

Courtesy of StockCharts.com

Courtesy of StockCharts.com

Courtesy of StockCharts.com

Courtesy of StockCharts.com

HE STUDIED stock charts in downtrends:

Courtesy of StockCharts.com

Courtesy of StockCharts.com

Courtesy of StockCharts.com

Courtesy of StockCharts.com

Courtesy of StockCharts.com

NEW TRADER only wanted to trade stocks that had charts with solid, stable uptrends in price. He decided it would be too stressful to trade stocks that had large, daily price swings.

Volatility was not going to be his friend in a trend trading system. He knew it would cause false stop losses to be triggered when the stock briefly broke below support, and early profit taking when the price would momentarily reverse below the trailing stop. A volatile stock could lose its 10-day moving average one day and be back over it again the next day.

New Trader wanted stocks that the 10-day moving averages held for at least 10 trading days. He saw an opportunity to buy stocks on his watchlist at the 10-day moving average, when it was breached and didn't recover before the close.

In uptrending stocks, by the time the 10-day was breached, price could run up 20% or more. He could let profits run, and with his watchlist in hand, he felt confident that he was on the right track when it came to effective system building.

He created some technical trading rules to guide him:

He would buy stocks on his watchlist as they trended up through the 10-day moving average or bounced off it as support.

After he made the buy, he would set a stop loss 5% below his purchase price. This would risk only 1% of his trading capital on an individual trade, with a 20% position size of his total trading capital.

Once his buy was correct and his stock started trending 5% above the 10-day moving average, he would set the stop at the current 10-day moving average, moving it up or down as needed. The popular moving average would be his trailing stop loss to lock in profits, and his sell signal when the trend reversed.

This system was based on taking profits when the uptrend ended. It played it safe, getting out before any large losses could accrue after the loss of key support levels.

He decided to trade \$2,000 per trade out of his \$10,000 account. He knew this would calm his nerves and let him focus on the system instead of the profits. He would increase his position size as his trading account grew. This would also help with risk; he knew the stocks could experience the 'torpedo' effect and fall quickly if they missed earnings. To limit risk, it would be important to keep his position size at 20% of his account and stop losses at the 10-day moving average.

New Trader's plan was starting to take shape.

He knew that his buy point would be important; he didn't want to be whip-sawed if a stock fell as soon as he bought, and he thought an initial of 5% in the stock's range would filter out most of the random noise.

His system was likely to trade well in if the market stayed in an uptrend. He was reminded of how different it was when real money was on the line and a stock didn't move upwards like he thought it would. This caused him to go back and add one more rule; He would only trade this system when the S&P 500 chart had the 10-day moving average above the 20-day moving average, and the price of the S&P 500 was above the 50-day moving average. The market needed to be in an overall uptrend and bullish for his system to be consistently profitable. He believed this rule would increase his odds substantially.

Now he felt confident in his system and thought that it would be successful. It enabled him to limit risk while keeping his emotions under control. He thought that he had created an edge, assisted by the many books he had read, the intense study of chart patterns, and the hours spent with Rich Trader.

His chart pattern studies had yielded him the greatest insight. He could almost visualize traders making decisions inside the charts he poured over. He could imagine them letting their profits run as stocks shot upwards in price, going higher and higher with little selling pressure.

He noticed fear in some charts as the uptrend was broken, and a stock quickly fell to its 20-day moving average, tumbling down to a longer term moving average like the 50-day. He knew that other traders were waiting patiently down there to bargain shop.

He reasoned that many moving averages could be self-fulfilling prophecies and were significant because market participants were watching them. He didn't think that the indicators themselves had real power, but the traders' belief in them influenced their buy and sell decisions.

It looked like traders repeatedly added to their positions at the 10-day moving average during strong uptrends. Even the 20-day, 50day, and the 100-day moving averages weren't immune to their decisions of buying to support prices or selling when these supports were broken.

He wondered if mutual fund managers have huge piles of cash sitting on the sidelines, waiting to enter these stocks that are under accumulation on pullbacks.

New Trader was confident his new system would capture

uptrends in the hottest stocks in the market. His watchlist would be stocks of the best companies; businesses whose future looked bright, and those that exceeded earnings expectations. But he would trade only if the stocks had good price charts and investor interest. Most importantly, he would time his buys at high probability points, based on historical technical analysis.

He thought he had built a robust trading plan and system for capturing uptrends, but what would Rich Trader think?

"The sooner you realize you're trading against other traders and not just the stocks or the market, the better off you will be."

QUINT TATRO

Rich Trader's Tip:

Don't trade someone else's system, build your own. Customize it to fit the principles you have studied and those that you can believe in. Your system must match your own risk tolerance and return expectations. Be wary of straying from your trading plan, because a mistake that wipes out your profits can impede your ability to trade going forward, and take a toll on your confidence. Don't let fear or greed make you do something destructive; always stick to your plan.

Recommended reading:

"The Complete Turtle Trader" by Michael Covel

SEVENTEEN

New Traders don't know when to cut losses or lock in gains; Rich Traders have an exit plan.

NEW TRADER GAVE Rich Trader some breathing room for a couple of weeks in hopes that he wasn't becoming annoying. He loved learning from Rich Trader because he didn't tell him what to do. Instead, he showed him how to do it and gave him powerful tips and tools he could use to become a better trader.

While styles of trading could differ, and systems could have different buy and sell signals, New Trader knew that the fundamental skills he was learning would make him successful in trading and in life.

He knew that a trading style and trading system are personal choices which must fit a trader's personality and tolerance for risk. Just because a system worked well for Rich Trader, didn't mean New

Trader could plug it in and find success. This made him keenly interested to know what Rich Trader thought about the plan New Trader had created for himself.

He felt different as he approached Rich Trader's front door. He couldn't put his finger on what it was, but he felt good. He had more control over his trading and his emotions. He wasn't obsessed with trading, or being glued to a screen. His goal was to make money and he didn't feel like he had to prove anything to anyone.

He knew that if he had to cut a loss, it was because the market was not conducive to his system at that time. He wasn't wrong and there was no reason to take it personally. If he followed his trading plan and had to take a loss, it was the cost of doing business.

He felt confident and calm. He felt like he was ready to start his career in the markets, and be a disciplined trader. As he waited for Rich Trader to answer the door, he realized that he felt like he had become a real trader, and he was about to have his first conversation with Rich Trader as a peer.

"Long time no see," Rich Trader said as he answered the door. "I was starting to think you gave up."

"Give up?" New Trader grinned. "I was just giving you a well-deserved vacation!"

"I have been asked to mentor many others over the years, and nine out of ten give up very quickly. Most don't even meet a second time. Their heads spin from all the information, and they are usually after easy money. The one thing I have learned in my decades in the market is that there is no easy money laying around. Believe me, I've searched everywhere." Rich Trader said very sternly before breaking out into booming laughter.

"Business is business, whether I'm trading stocks or delivering pizza. I understand that now. Success at anything in life requires controlling risk, the right mindset, a successful method, supply and demand, discipline, courage, limiting losses, and letting winners run.

The funny thing is, the principles you have been teaching me for trading have also been helping me in other areas. I think more clearly about many aspects of my life, and my journal has become a self-help journal as well as a trading journal. I would like to read you some thoughts from my notes and see what you think."

Rich Trader nodded, and New Trader began reading. He was excited to share the observations with his mentor.

"In life, as in trading, the right mindset is crucial for success. You must be confident in your decisions because they are based on cause and effect, not on emotions or opinions. Negative people who are unsure of themselves are not successful in any field. You need faith in yourself and your methods to persevere and not give up before you are successful.

You can risk too much and lose it all in your business, life, marriage, friendships, or family. You must measure the potential cost of every action. One affair can cost you your marriage, just like a big trade with too much risk can cost you all your capital.

In business, there are methods that bring in customers and turn a profit, and others that can run off customers and lose money. Trading is similar, and methods that turn a consistent and long-term profit are essential for success.

Having unrealistic expectations in a marriage, job, or business will lead to unhappiness and failure, just like it will in trading. You must set realistic expectations so you don't get discouraged easily and quit. You must be satisfied that the results are worth your effort over the long-term. You need to understand what to expect before you any endeavor.

Those who succeed are those who can most effectively manage stress. The best ways to manage stress are to only enter situations that you feel comfortable and knowledgeable about, and to progress slowly, only taking on additional risk and responsibility when you're sure that you're ready.

Patience can pay big dividends in life. Patience is not inaction; it's knowing what you're looking for and acting at the right time. Whether you're waiting for the right trade setup or the right person to marry, patience can protect you from irrational emotions and feelings. Wait for what you want, and when it's there, go get it.

In life, as in trading, people with a written plan accomplish more than people without a plan. When you're calm and rational, write down the goals you want to pursue. This will provide you with a map when life circumstances bring out your fears, greed, and other destructive emotions.

Education doesn't end in school. To be successful in trading, as in life, we can't stop learning. The market and the world are constantly advancing and changing, and the only way to keep up is to keep learning.

In life, most gamblers are broke and most of good business owners become rich. This also applies in trading.

In life, if you risk everything enough times, you will eventually lose everything. Instead, try to move in the direction of your goals every day. Even with setbacks, in the long run you'll realize your goals.

Before you make any decision in life, you should ask the question: "What do I have to lose?" This should precede, "What do I have to gain?" If the answer is: I could lose $100, but if I'm right I could gain $500 and my odds of being right are 50%, this is a good risk/reward profile. If it's reversed, then you have a bad risk/reward scenario and should pass. Again, this also applies to life in general.

Failure to admit when you're wrong can be disastrous. When you're going down the wrong road, it's better to turn around sooner rather than later. Never fight a war when there is nothing worth fighting for, because even if you win, you'll be left with the regret of what it cost you.

Have an exit plan in place, and take your profits when you win big. If your house goes from $100,000 to $300,000 in a short amount of time, have a plan to sell and move. Don't wait and let it drop back down to $100,000. Many people are at the right place at the right time and win what is equivalent to the lottery in stocks, a house, or a business, but have no exit plan. They ride it all the way up, and then all the way down again with nothing to show for it. Always have a plan to take the money off the table.

What separates successful people from unsuccessful people in all areas of life is that they persevere until they are successful. Everyone must overcome failures, but those who keep going are the ones with successful marriages, businesses, careers, and trading systems. Resilience doesn't guarantee you will win, but it gives you more opportunities to succeed because you stay in the game.

People who are successful become experts in one area, rather than a jack of all trades and a master of none. They usually put in at least 10 years or 10,000 hours to learn and master one business, one career, one marriage, or one trading style.

Successful people do what leads to success, not what they think will make them successful. They read books, study patterns, have mentors, and learn cause and effect.

Winners base their actions on processes that have led to proven results, not on their own opinions or predictions. Feedback is crucial to them, unlike people with strong opinions who think they can predict what will happen. These types frequently reject feedback. Winners go with the flow of the trend that leads to their success.

In life, those who are driven by their vision, passion, and plan usually end up where they want to be, or close to it. Those who let their emotions and feelings take over and drive their decision-making process usually end up somewhere less ideal.

People who realize they have made a mistake and cut their losses quickly will be more successful than people who waste years on a situation that continuously gets worse. It's equally as important to continue in a situation that is successful until that trend changes."

"I see you've been listening. I think you may be starting to teach me a few things. I'm very impressed." Rich Trader beamed.

"Thank you. It's all starting to come together for me. You've made me think about many principles of success that I never thought about before. That does make me wonder what you have found to be the most difficult part of being a trader? What did you learn the most from?"

"I've always hated to lose, and particularly hate losing money. It used to make me feel bad about myself and my future. Now I realize it's the cost of doing business, but I still don't like it. This character trait caused me to make some bad decisions as young trader. I rebelled against taking that first stop loss, and more than once, I allowed a small loss to turn into a large one. I learned my lesson the hard way.

My first year of trading, I planned to get out of a trade with a $100 loss. I thought I was lucky because I didn't take a loss on a couple of occasions. I watched a $115 loss go back to even, and then a $150 loss turn into a $100 profit, so this emboldened me. As it turned out, I wasn't lucky. I was unlucky because it took me longer to tame my ego and discipline myself to take the first loss. It was difficult to keep myself from thinking that I would get lucky again. The next time I was down $100, I abandoned my plan, thinking that I was smart enough to read the price and volume action in real time. Any young trader in that situation is only going to see what he wants to see. I didn't want to take the loss, then I didn't want to be wrong about not taking it.

Then I committed the deadly sin of a trader, I hoped it would get back to even. This was the worst trade I ever made. I turned what should have been a trade of a few days for a $300 profit into a week-long ordeal that turned a $100 loss into a $500 loss. Just as bad as the monetary loss was the ridiculous amount of time I wasted glued to every tick. I rode an emotional roller for a week, and it was completely unnecessary. That experience taught me to honor my stops when they were hit the first time. The first planned stop loss is the best one to follow. I promised myself that I would never do that again, and that I would try to implement that lesson in the rest of my life. Taking your first planned stop in any situation avoids emotional wear and tear, and saves your most precious resource, time. These are important for a long trading career."

"A loss never bothers me after I take it. I forget it overnight. But being wrong – not taking the loss – that is what does damage to the pocketbook and to the soul."

JESSE LIVERMORE

Rich Trader's Tip:

Always have a reason to get into a trade, and then a reason to get out of one. Having a trading plan gives you an edge over the traders that rely on emotion, predictions, and opinions to make trading decisions. When you get trapped in a losing trade it's usually an emotional mistake rather than one of intelligence. It can be difficult for a trader to learn to lose, but you must accept the loss and move on. The smaller you keep your trades at the beginning, the easier it will be to accept a losing trade and exit. The larger the amount of money you will lose on the exit, the more a trade can be influenced by ego, stress, and destructive emotions.

Recommended reading:

"Wall Street: The Other Las Vegas" by Nicolas Darvas

EIGHTEEN

New Traders cut profits short and let losses run; Rich Traders let profits run and cut losses short.

THIS WAS the moment of truth. Rich Trader was looking over New Trader's system.

New Trader only visited his mentor every other week instead of several times a week, until finally months had passed since he last asked for guidance from Rich Trader. The decrease in his visits wasn't a lack of commitment. New Trader spent at least two hours a day, every day, looking at charts, studying his watchlist, and reading the best trading books he could find. He knew that Rich Trader taught him the fundamentals, but it was up to him to build his future.

Like many new traders, he was initially disappointed that Rich Trader didn't show him the holy grail of trading, the yellow brick road that led to guaranteed profits. His preconceived ideas of how a professional trader operated, had also been shattered. He had expected a multi-screen setup, financial news scrolling by in the background, with his mentor agonizing over ever tick. Instead, he had learned that there was no holy grail, and no free money. It required a lot of hard work, research, and a plan that was customized to the trader. And that the goal was to work smarter, not necessarily harder.

New Trader waited patiently as Rich Trader continued to look over his trading plan, his system, and the records of his previous paper trades. He had settled on trend trading and he was eager to hear what his mentor thought of his track record.

"Your winning ratio looks very good – 60%. That's excellent. However, your system was benefiting from the recent uptrend in the market. Your losses were small due to your tight stops, but that may be too tight; you could experiment with 3% stops under the 10-day moving average as your stop, or even use a 20-day moving average as a better stop loss level. When the market turns choppy, or at the beginning of a downtrend, it will significantly affect your winning ratio. But it will also give you fewer trades, as the 10-day moving average will likely become resistance and give few buy signals. I also think your system will take you safely to cash in a major market retracement. This is a good plan to limit big losses if you're on the wrong side of the market during a correction."

New Trader was so set on the 10-day moving average that he had never even considered any others to give himself more flexibility during periods of volatility. What if another moving average showed more reaction than the 10-day or 20-day? This was something to consider.

Rich Trader continued looking over his paper trades with considerable interest.

"Your payoff ratio was a little over 2:1. You made about $200 in profits for every $100 in losses. This is excellent; it will be less when you begin to trade with real money and must figure in the difference of the bid/ask spread when entering and exiting trades, along with commissions and slippage. You likely won't get the price you want so easily, especially with market orders on stocks with lower volume at different times in the trading day. But a payoff ratio of 2:1 is still a very robust and profitable system, and you should do well in the long-term, especially during bull markets. You'll make money being correct half of the time if you continue to keep your losses small."

"Yes, paper trading is like shooting fish in a barrel. I'm ready to start building a real trading record. I think it's ready to go live." New Trader said confidently.

"Your largest winning trade was $500, and your largest losing trade was $125. That looks very good. This is an amazing return for a $2,500 trade. You had a $25 stock move up to $30 without touching the 10-day moving average? You're definitely trading stocks with good momentum and investor interest."

"I sold the big winner at $30 when it pulled back to the 10-day moving average on the chart; it pulled back to $30 after a runaway trend. It ran up before the company's earnings announcement to as high as $33.50. My system had me sell this stock and take profits before the announcement, and it fell back to $25 after the earnings were announced.

That experience makes me want to add a rule that I don't hold through earnings. The trend can swing significantly either way after these high fliers announce their earnings for the quarter. The stocks can even crash after their company's report blows out earnings above expectations; it's just a matter of when the stock runs out of new buyers, and if the good earnings are already baked into the stock's price."

"That would be a great rule to better manage risk and volatility. While you may give up some profits, it will help you avoid the extreme risk and equity drawdowns that could happen when holding through a risk event. I always put capital preservation before capital appreciation. When I traded individual stocks, I only held through earnings once, and that was a disaster. I had much better risk adjusted returns playing the expectation of earnings leading up to the announcement than I did holding through earnings. It was like the Wild West after an earnings announcement and very unpredictable.

Your average winning trade was $212 and your average losing trade was $105. These are strong numbers. So, you returned 42.6% on your $10,000 in capital in 50 trades? That's impressive, but real trading will shave that down dramatically. The market may enter a bear market at the exact moment you start trading this system, causing multiple stops to be hit in a row, resulting in several losses. Commissions will take a bite out of every trade, especially with your trading size. Twenty dollars in commission on a $2,500 trade is 0.8% on the capital, before you know if you win or lose. You need to trade with a per share broker who charges about $1 per 100 shares, and not one who charges $10 per trade or your account will be eaten up with commissions.

You will also experience technical problems at the worst possible times, including issues with your computer, the Internet, the power company, or your broker's web site or trading platform. When this happens, you may miss a great trade which would have made you a lot of money. You will also place market orders that are filled at worse prices than you expected. When these things happen, and they will, they will hurt your returns, challenge your patience, and make you angry. At these moments it's important to stay calm and follow your plan.

A 42.6% return in 50 trades may be a little too good to be true. If you get a bigger account size or a cheaper broker, I think your system is an excellent starting point. I would expect a return in the lower double digits during uptrending bull markets, probably around 20%-25% after all factors are taken into consideration. Your system will likely lose at the beginning of a bear market until it no longer has buy signals, and until the next uptrend begins."

New Trader had a lot to think about. He knew what Rich Trader said was true. "Would you suggest I develop a second system to trade in a bear market?"

"If you like, it's up to you, but some traders don't ever like to short. They would rather buy stocks that are in uptrends in bear markets like gold mines, oil stocks, consumer staples, energy stocks, discount stores, or just stay in cash and wait. That is a personal choice. The longer I trade, the less I see a lot of value in shorting the stock market. Most back tests show the short side adds little value due to false signals. All of my long-term returns and capital gains have been on the long side. A short can only go to zero and give you a 100% return, but on the long side a stock can double, triple, or more. The asymmetry favors the long side for returns, because the long-term trend of the market is up."

"That would double my chances to make money." New Trader said, hesitantly.

"It also doubles your chances to lose money," Rich Trader replied.

"So, I am at my starting point? I am ready to begin real trading?"

Rich Trader put his hand on New Trader's shoulder and smiled broadly.

"You're more than ready. The only thing that's left is for you to learn from what the markets teach you; they give great feedback and they're never wrong. Prices are always correct, because they are the composite of what every buyer and seller agrees to pay at that moment. The challenge is to be able to profit from the next path that price takes in a trend or a range."

"I don't know if I'm graduating from stock trading college or stock trading boot camp."

"Well, one thing is for sure, you're going to battle others to be successful. If you do all the things you have learned, you will profit from others' mistakes."

On that day, New Trader decided that he would keep trading until he was successful.

He was no longer a new trader, he was a trend trader.

"It's not whether you're right or wrong that's important, but

how much money you make when you're right and how much you lose when you're wrong."

GEORGE SOROS

My Golden Rules of Trading:

- Never add to a losing trade.
- Don't lose more than 1% to 2% of your trading capital on a single trade.
- Don't trade something you don't understand 100%.
- Trade in the direction of the trend in your trading time frame.
- Only look for low risk/high reward trades or high probability setups.
- Trade your plan, your system, your signals, the chart, and price action, rather than opinions, bias, or predictions.
- Trade the correct methodology that fits your personality.
- Don't trade unless you have a plan with rules on entries, exits, and risk management.
- Trade like each trade is one of the next 100.
- Don't give up!

Recommended reading:

"5 Moving Average Signals That Beat Buy and Hold: Back tested Stock Market Signals" by Steve Burns and Holly Burns

WANT TO LEARN MORE?

Join thousands of other trading students at New Trader University! Our eCourses are created especially for those just starting out in the markets.

New Trader 101 – The place to start for new traders

In the New Trader 101 eCourse, you'll get:

-13 high quality videos covering how and why to trade

-Real trade examples with detailed charts

-The most powerful trading psychology and stress management techniques being offered today.

Join New Trader 101 today!

Moving Averages 101 – Everything you need to know to harness the power of Moving Averages!

In the Moving Averages 101 eCourse, you'll get:

-11 high quality videos covering how to get started with Moving Averages

-Real trade examples

-More than 45 annotated charts

Join Moving Averages 101 today!

Price Action Trading 101 – Master the concepts of reactive technical analysis, and learn the best times to get in and out of your trades!

In the Price Action Trading 101 eCourse, you'll get:

-17 high quality videos covering the best way to enter and exit your trades for a profit.

-Step-by-step examples

-More than 30 annotated charts

Join Price Action Trading 101 today!

Options 101 –

This 19-part video course is packed with information about Options, and how they can help you up your trading game. It includes real trading examples, many visuals, and an Options Play Strategy Guide that you won't find anywhere else.

In the Options 101 eCourse, you'll get:

-19 high quality videos covering how and why to trade

-Step-by-step trading examples

-Many annotated charts

Join Options 101 today!

Did you enjoy this eBook?

Please consider writing a review.

Listen to many of our titles on Audible!

Read more of our bestselling titles:

So You Want to be a Trader
New Trader 101
Moving Averages 101
Buy Signals and Sell Signals
Trading Habits
Investing Habits
Calm Trader

ABOUT THE AUTHORS

Steve Burns started investing in 1993, and trading his own accounts in 1995. It was love at first trade. A natural teacher with a unique ability to cut through the bull and make complex ideas simple, Steve wrote New Trader Rich Trader and started NewTraderU.com in 2011 to help new traders survive and thrive in the markets.

When Holly met Steve in 2014, she knew they could take his trading knowledge to the next level. As CTO, Holly has helped Steve publish 12 best-selling books, four popular eCourses, and created an extensive social media community.

For more information:
www.NewTraderU.com
stephen@newtraderu.com

Made in the USA
Middletown, DE
09 September 2020